ALL THE DYING VOICES

Reginald Edmund

BROADWAY PLAY PUBLISHING INC
New York
www.broadwayplaypublishing.com
info@broadwayplaypublishing.com

First edition: May 2025
I S B N: 978-0-88145-906-7

Book design: Marie Donovan
Page make-up: Adobe InDesign
Typeface: Palatino

The City of the Bayou Collection is a series of nine plays. They are the playwright's attempt at making a contemporary House of Atreus through a Afro-Surrealist lens. The plays, in order, are:

THE DAUGHTERS OF THE MOON*

SOUTHBRIDGE*

IN THE PROPHET'S HOUSE

BLOOD ON THE BAYOU

REDEMPTION OF ALLAH BLACK

JUNETEENTH STREET*

THE ORDAINED SMILE OF SAINT SADIE MAY JENKINS*

THE LAST CADILLAC

ALL THE DYING VOICES*

published by Broadway Play Publishing Inc

CHARACTERS & SETTING

HARRISON JUST, *30s, Black male, District Attorney for the City of Houston*

OFFICER CRIS HELLER, *late 20s / 30s, White male, police officer*

LIL J (JAXSON PRICE), *late teens, Black male*

DAEJAH / PROTESTOR, *late teens, Black female*

OFFICER TOMMS, *late 30s/40s, Black male, police officer*

MOMMA (JAMILLA PRICE), *late 40s-50s, Black female*

REVEREND MCHENRY, *late 50-60s, Black female*

MAYOR LEE & CORONER, *late 40s, Black female*

CAPITÁN & PROTESTOR 2, *late 50-70s, Black male*

NEWSCASTER 1, NEWSCASTER 2, & NEWSCASTER 3 *should always be seen in shadows, and played by various members cast.*

The play takes place in various parts of Houston, Texas. A playground, a jail, an interrogation room, the home of HARRISON JUST *and the church of* REVEREND MCHENRY.

NOTE

Gaps in dialogue should be considered a breath or a moment. The longer the gap the longer the pause.

"…" means silence

"—" means they are cut off before finishing their statement

Actors should perform this piece at a fevered pace. I encourage directors to consider that roles of the newscasters, protestors can be performed by doubling, and I urge them to be bold in experimentation with videos projections, social media postings or other means of communication. At the same time I want to remind directors to remember that this is theatre, steer away from the big set with massive design and keep close to the basis of storytelling. This could all be done on a bare stage. Scenes move and weave together, past and present collide.

ACT ONE

First Theme

(Darkness…the sound of a heart beating…faster and faster it beats. Lightning flashes once…twice…three times lightning flashes and we see a young man [LIL J] tangled upon a swing set, chains wrapped around his hands and neck. Body twisted and contorted as a shadowy figure of a woman [DAEJAH] stands in the background reaching out towards him. Another man stands watching as well [CAPITÁN]. Hands rise from the earth, reaching for LIL J. Lightning flashes. An image flashes the words "All the Dying Voices" upon a screen.)

(Black out)

Second Theme

(A chorus of journalists report on the boy's death early.)

REPORTER 1: A teenager found hanged in the predominately black neighborhood of Fourth Ward, lovingly referred to as Freedman's Town.

REPORTER 2: Youth found hanged in a playground in 4th Ward, a police officer found at the scene has been brought in for questioning.

REPORTER 3: African American teen found hanging from playground swings. Community wants answers. More news to come.

(The sound of crowd growing followed by the sound, of a gavel banging three times. Lights shift, and HARRISON *dressed in suit and tie is standing in the mayor's office. The mayor eats a cookie. The sound of angry voices can be heard outside.)*

MAYOR: I'm cheating on my wife with baked goods. I always thought if I ever stray from that woman it would be some sweet looking intern with perky tits and a fluffy ass. But no...no luck for me. Its baked goods. I know its shit for my diabetes but hell they're so damn delicious.

HARRISON: Your secret is safe with me.

MAYOR: It damn well better be.

HARRISON: You know you're a twisted woman. Most people would never talk to their subordinate like this.

MAYOR: No, I'm a powerful woman and that's the difference, darling. Besides if I can't show my friends my true me what's the point of it all.
Speaking of wives, how's yours? Still pregnant?

HARRISON: Still pregnant.

MAYOR: Don't know how she does it. Having something move into her body, feeding on her. Gives me the willies just thinking about it.

HARRISON: You're so maternal. You wanted to talk to me, mayor?

MAYOR: Yeah, sorry, come on in... What's going on with this case...umm, the hanging case with the kid?

HARRISON: We're piecing everything together now. Look Mayor, I appreciate you having faith in me to handle this but maybe I'm not the right guy to be prosecuting this case. I have a smart new assistant that's looking for a chance to herself—

MAYOR: I honestly can't think of a better damn
person for this case... Than you. You are a part of that
community. You grew up in that community. You rose
out of that community. They need to be able to see that
the one guiding the fair and balanced scales into Lady
Justice's hands is someone that looks just like them.

HARRISON: I understand that but—

MAYOR: No *buts*! The election is in two weeks. Fourteen
damn days. Three hundred thirty six hours. I can
hear the press going insane on this one now. "Mayor
Lee doesn't give a fuck about her black community!".
Especially after all the reports have come out lately...I
want you to give us the answers we need on this one.
We need to get ahead of this.
Take care of this one for me. I will not have them say
this city was fine when we had a white mayor, now
look at the mess we're in. These white people will
not attempt to Obama me. Appease the police, make
sure the blacks in Fourth Ward don't burn down my
goddamn city, and get me a bad guy. You hear me.
My job is on the fucking line, and if my job is on the
fucking line that means your job is on the fucking line.
You understand me? Two weeks can you do that?

HARRISON: I'm sorry I can't do that. I want to leave my
mark. I'm not going to achieve that with a case like
this.

MAYOR: I don't think you understood me.

HARRISON: I understand you just fine, Madame Mayor,
we got too many unanswered questions here to do my
job. Too many variables. I'm overloaded on cases as it
is.

MAYOR: Harrison. Harrison. Harrison.

HARRISON: I really hate it when you do that.

MAYOR: I want you… No, I need you personally on this case.

HARRISON: You need someone who cares…and frankly as horrible as what occurred might be I don't.
I have much more high-profile cases that need to be handled.

MAYOR: Harrison, I never took you to be the dense one. Let me be clear…I want this either looked at as a clean kill or you throw that fucker into a dark cave never to be seen or heard from again. You got me? I don't care what happens you just make sure it's disappears by Election Day. Plain and simple. Cause I got things in motion. I need this to die away. We bring crime down in that 4th Ward, it's going to attract businesses, its going to attract the right kind of people. That's going to raise the tax base, and that means more revenue. And after what this city has been through with Hurricane Harvey this city needs revenue, this city needs urban renewal. We need this Jaxson Price incident to go away and go away now. That whole Eric Strong murder six years ago, was the death of the last mayor's career, and I'll be damned if I get sent packing over the same damn thing.

HARRISON: I hear you.

MAYOR: Good.

HARRISON: But…

MAYOR: Ah, shit.

HARRISON: If I do this then I want something from you.

MAYOR: You want my seat?

HARRISON: It looks really comfy. I clean this up. I want your endorsement for me as mayor after your next term is up.

MAYOR: That's really what you want? My endorsement?

HARRISON: Full endorsement.

MAYOR: Prove yourself with this one. Play the game Harrison and play it to win. Find the truth before this city explodes and my endorsement is yours.

HARRISON: Fine… Give me the file.

(The MAYOR *hands* HARRISON *the file regarding the case.)*

HARRISON: This is everything?

MAYOR: Police report, coroners… It's all there. Everything you need.
Now get the hell out of my office.

HARRISON & MAYOR: The clock is ticking.

*(*HARRISON *loosens his tie. Looks out towards the audience)*

HARRISON: Those words echo through my mind. I felt it. That clock weighing down on me. Strangling me. Two weeks before Election Day. Two weeks before this city explodes. Two weeks to get justice for a young boy, or exonerate a cop. So much at stake. So much that could be lost.

(Lights sweep the stage clear. Leaving only HARRISON *standing alone.* LIL J *appears in the park. The two eye each other before* HARRISON *turns and leaves.)*

Second Movement

(The sound of a jail cell opening)

*(*HARRISON *sits at a table, opens his brief case and pulls out pen and paper.* OFFICER HELLER *enters, he's in uniform. He's nervous.)*

HARRISON: Hello. Officer Cris Heller? You are Cris, right? Is it alright if I call you Cris? Sorry I'm late.

A great deal of people wanted to set up this meeting before I make the decision whether to prosecute you or not. So, for now... You're not charged with anything... yet. Do you understand what you've been accused of?

HELLER: ...

HARRISON: Cris? Do you understand what you are— Look, I understand that you're scared but I need you to work with me on this. I'm here...talking to you now...instead of processing paperwork because very powerful people said that I need to make this sit happen. The mayor's office is taking this situation extremely serious. We're hoping you can provide us with the truth of what happened that night.

HELLER: Can we just...
Can we just get this over with?

HARRISON: I suppose so. So I had the chance to go through your records. It's impressive. Two tours of duty in Iraq. A few reprimands here and there for U S Code 2579, but other than that your file is filled with high marks of recommendations. You were a regular Rambo over there weren't you? Ah, you got to pardon my ignorance but what's U S Code 2579 mean? I'm not familiar with military law.

HELLER: I was reprimanded for inappropriate recording on the retaining of battlefield objects. Stupid mistake with paperwork. It's silly really.

HARRISON: Liked your trophies huh?

HELLER: I was young. I had a fascination with collecting things from my time in a warzone. It was nothing major. A bullet here, a gun there...Like I said it was stupid...I straightened up. I don't understand, what does that have to do with this case?

HARRISON: It doesn't. I just was curious about the small marks on your otherwise golden record...Shall we move on? Let's start. Are you alright in here? How are you?

HELLER: They let me put on my uniform to meet with you. I guess that's pretty good, right?
I get to sit in solitary confinement cause if the animals find out I'm a cop they'll rip me apart. What else you want me to say?

HARRISON: Look Cris, let me just start by saying that I know that you are in a very complicated situation here. An extremely complicated situation. And if you…if we don't talk this out right now it could steam roll you…I have a single job. Find the truth and bring justice. If you don't talk to me then I can only rely on the truths of every other person but you. Talk to me. Can you do that? Talk to me. We want to help you.

HELLER: So generous of you.

HARRISON: Look, Heller. You're accused of killing a kid—

HELLER: I know what your accusing me of!
I didn't even know the damn kid, alright.
(He touches his neck uncomfortably.)

HARRISON: Your reports say otherwise.

HELLER: I didn't know him.
(He touches his neck again.)
I just want to go home.
And this… This…what you all are doing to me is bullshit.
I've been on the force less than a year and the city just throws me under the bus like this. Seven months I've patrolled those streets, seven months I've made sure people stayed safe in that community. I've worked my ass off to keep garbage off the streets and help god-fearing tax paying citizens live their lives. What more you want from me?

(*Silence. Awkward silence*)

HARRISON: And what about the kind of people like Jaxson Price? He the garbage you work so hard to keep off the streets?

HELLER: Man, I'm innocent. You guys parading me around like I'm some kind of bad guy. I shouldn't be sitting in a god damn jail cell over this. I had nothing to do with his death. Alright. I'm a good cop, I'm a Christian, I've served this country and most of all I'm fuckin' innocent! I'm innocent!! I'm innocent!!!

HARRISON: Calm down. Calm down Officer Heller. I'm just here to get your side of the story.

HELLER: Nah, you're not here to get my side of the story. People have already made up their minds. I can tell by how they look at me.

HARRISON: The way they look at you?

HELLER: Yeah, the same way that you are looking at me right now. Like I'm some kind of dirty cop. Let's throw him to the wolves. Is what they're saying?

HARRISON: And are you?

HELLER: Am I what?

HARRISON: A dirty cop?

HELLER: …

HARRISON: Look my job is simple. Find out what happened. Get justice for that kid's death? And if your innocent get you the hell out of here. That's my job. What was your relation to the victim, Jaxson Price?

HELLER: I told you, I didn't know him.
(*Again, he clutches at his neck.*)

HARRISON: You alright?

HELLER: Yeah…yeah, I'm fine. Just need some water that's all. Look, he was just some kid on my beat.

HARRISON: Approximately how many times have you had encounters with Jaxson during your beats?

HELLER: I don't know…once or twice maybe…I mean he was just a nobody kid.

HARRISON: You typically stand and scream under hung bodies of nobody kids?

HELLER: I was… I became…distressed I've never seen something like that before. I mean I've seen a little bit of every kind of crazy imaginable in this life time… you know cause of the…
(He points to his badge.)
…but I've…I've never seen something like that…just hanging like that.
The chains around him…body just swinging' in the wind…those eyes… Never seen something like that. It was unsettling you know. Can I go now?

HARRISON: Let me ask you one last thing, Officer Heller. Did you kill Jaxson Price?

HELLER: I didn't hang that boy.

(Lights shift and swirl.)

(LIL J appears on the playground carrying a small backpack filled with D V Ds and C Ds. It's night time. He digs up his stash of money and adds another wad of cash to it. There is the sound of wind chimes and a teenage girl appears from the darkness sneaks up on him, puts her finger to his back like it's a gun.)

DAEJAH: Give me all your money.
(She laughs.)
Oh shit, you should've seen ya face just now. Swear you looked like ya just shit ya pants.

LIL J: Damnit Daejah!!!
Uhhh, I hate you so much. Daejah, that shits not funny.

DAEJAH: Nah, negro, it's hella funny, you must have jumped like thirty feet, J baby.

LIL J: I knew it was you. With that funky old dollar store perfume, you always wearing. I smelled you a mile away.

DAEJAH: Whatever, jackass you know like my perfume.

LIL J: Nah girl, you smell…I like you natural. That's what I like.

DAEJAH: Boy, whatever, what you know? You stupid. Anyway, you got to put your money somewhere better than that, J Baby, one day someone is going to snatch it if you not careful.

LIL J: Oh, is that what you plannin' steal my money, run off without me?

DAEJAH: Negro, please, you still wearing my necklace?

Lil J shows off his necklace.

LIL J: Never taking it off til the day I die.

DAEJAH: Well as long as you are wearing that, I think it should be clear as day, that I ain't plannin' on runnin' nowhere without you.

LIL J: Good answer.

DAEJAH: Damn straight, it's a good answer.

LIL J: I was wondering if you were going to show up? What took you so long this time?

DAEJAH: Boy, you see me here every other day, every week, for the last two months, don't ask dumb questions. You know I'm all about that C P Time! Makes you appreciate all this sexy so much more… Anyway, how come you don't take me nowhere? You can't take me nowhere special, why we always meet at this dirty ass park?

LIL J: Hey, I like this playground. Just like to… Just like to…get away you know. Come here to think.

DAEJAH: What are you thinkin'?

LIL J: Dunno
Just thinkin'. Sometimes I just sit here and listen.

DAEJAH: Listen to what?

LIL J: Nothing…kinda too hard to explain.

Anyhow its nothing…come here.

DAEJAH: What?

LIL J: Don't 'what' me! Come here, girl.

(DAEJAH *comes closer.* LIL J *kisses her.)*

DAEJAH: Lame. You call that a kiss?

LIL J: Shut up. I can't stand you.

DAEJAH: You betta love the hell outta me. Cause one day you gonna look for me and this pretty behind of mine is gonna be gone…ghost.

LIL J: Where you gonna go?

DAEJAH: That's for me to know and you to find out. If you sweet to me, maybe I'll take you with me.

LIL J: Oh yeah?

DAEJAH: Yeah.

(DAEJAH *and* LIL J *kiss.)*

LIL J: Come here. Look at this.

DAEJAH: That has to be… That's gotta be hundreds of dollars.

LIL J: Six. If I counted right. Maybe if you sweet on me I'll take you with me.
When I get the hell outta this place.

DAEJAH: Oh really?

LIL J: Really.

(DAEJAH *and* LIL J *kiss.*)

DAEJAH: Well, one…I hope you know I don't need your money for me to get on outta here. If and when I feel like getting' outta here. I will.
And two… You best not be doing anything to get your ass in trouble.

LIL J: I mean T has been wanting me to connect with him—

DAEJAH: You not going to do it, right?

LIL J: What I look like?

DAEJAH: You really want me to answer that?

LIL J: Nah, not my thing, just doing the bootleg movie hustle, true entre-po-negro for real that's me.
I've been saving up, babe, I've been saving up and we gonna get outta here. I promise you that.
I just got to lockdown maybe two, three hundred dollars, maybe a little bit more and we can get outta here. Leave this city and anywhere you wanna go.

DAEJAH: Anywhere I want to go, huh?

LIL J: You name the place babe.

DAEJAH: Don't make promises that you can't keep, J.

(DAEJAH *and* LIL J *kiss.*)

LIL J: Let's get out of here. Let's go… Anywhere you want.

DAEJAH: That would be amazing.
I got to go. I just wanted to check up on you.
When you finally get the nerve up to say what I've been waiting for you to say,
I'll leave with you. Till then I ain't going nowhere.
I'll talk to you soon.
Keep out of trouble. I love you…

LIL J: I know.

DAEJAH: You suppose to say I love you back.

(LIL J *watches as* DAEJAH *leaves.*)

LIL J: I'm Lil' J, baby, I don't keep outta trouble. I am trouble!
(*He places his money into his hiding place.*)

(*As* LIL J *does so a beam of a flashlight sweeps over him.*)

(*A voice calls out. It's* HELLER *and* TOMMS.)

HELLER: Hey kid. Stay where you are.

(LIL J, *gets up, grabs his bag and tries to run but as he does so another officer grabs him and throws him to the ground.*)

TOMMS: Muthaphucka!!! Didn't he tell you to stay where you are?

(TOMMS *pins* LIL J *down to the ground.*)

HELLER: Hey, come on, come on he's just a kid.

(TOMMS *pulls out a flask and takes a drink.*)

TOMMS: Looks like a fuckin' animal you ask me. If he was just a kid, his ass would be at home doing homework. This right here ain't nothing but a mutt dog. Ain't that right? Quit being so damn soft, Heller.
(*He takes another sip from his flask.*)

HELLER: All I'm saying is ease up on him.

TOMMS: Look rookie you're new, but eventually you got to learn that if you want to clean up these streets, then you got to teach these idiots a lesson.

LIL J: Owww… What you do that to me for?!!

HELLER: What you trying to run for?

TOMMS: See what you made me do, kid?
Now who were you talking to? Where are they?

LIL J: Ain't nobody else here, man. Just me.

TOMMS: Just you?

LIL J: Yeah, it's just me… Get off me.

TOMMS: Check his bag. See what he got in there?

LIL J: Leave it! Leave my shit alone, man! It's mine.

TOMMS: Shut up.
(To HELLER*)*
Go on check it.

*(*HELLER *checks the bag.)*

HELLER: Nothing but a bunch of bootlegs D V Ds.

TOMMS: Let him up.
What the hell is wrong with you kid, don't you know
that's a felony?
You can get five years for this.

LIL J: Got to make a living somehow.

TOMMS: Then get a job a McDonalds, you little shit.

LIL J: Hey, hey, I know you.

*(*TOMMS *grabs* LIL J *by the collar and pulls him towards
him.)*

TOMMS: Nah, you don't know me. You don't want to
know me. But feel free to test me boy. I'm begging you
to.

LIL J: Asshole.

TOMMS: What you say to me?!!

*(*HELLER *steps in to intervene.)*

HELLER: How about I take you down to the precinct
have your mother come pick your smart ass up.

*(*TOMMS *throws* LIL J *to the ground.)*

HELLER: Jesus Christ, Tomms, He's just a kid.

TOMMS: Yeah, a little shit kid. Get up. I said get up.

You think I wanted to do that? You think I like beating
you up kid?

Now I'm feeling kind today. I'm feeling mighty damn
generous.

So, what I'm going to do is let you off with a warning.
Look kid, don't let me catch you out here at this park
after hours. You hear me?

Cause next time it's your ass.

*(He takes one of the D V Ds out of the bag and tosses it to
the ground before smashing it under his boot.)*

You're not worth the paperwork, kid. Get the hell out
of here.

(He drinks from the flask.)

HELLER: Hey kid,

*(*HELLER *tosses the bag of D V Ds to* LIL J)*

HELLER: don't forget your bag. Keep out of trouble,
alright.

(To TOMMS*)*

Was that necessary? He's just a kid.

TOMMS: You be in my shoes for a few more years
you'll see. You can't be nice to these people. As cops
we're targets, you understand that? They're out here.
Shooting us for no reason.

You're new but when you deal with these people you
got to remember you in a warzone. Don't mean to
alarm you but these are my people. Sick of feeling like
I'm always fighting my own people. Sick of seeing
them out here destroying themselves.

*(*HELLER *and* TOMMS *walk away as* LIL J *picks up the
shattered disc.)*

(A PROTESTOR *takes to the stage. Then another followed by
another. They march carrying signs calling for justice.)*

*(*HARRISON *visits the park. There's flowers, candles, and
cards, markings of memorial by the swing set.)*

HARRISON: Wandered during my lunch break from
my office downtown to the playground where Jaxson
Price took his last breath. Playgrounds in my mind are
places of joy. I'm not sure if this place ever knew that
word. The swing set is littered with cards, candles and
flowers in remembrance of the life snatched away far
to young. Why did I come here?

(CAPITÁN *enters.*)

CAPITÁN: Hey! Hey! Hey suit and tie! Yeah, ya there.
Ya lost?

HARRISON: No, I'm not lost.

CAPITÁN: Well, ya look lost to me, brethren.
Ya don't look like ya belong here if ya ask me.

HARRISON: You'd be surprised.
I grew up here in Freemans' Town.

CAPITÁN: Funny that name. Have us Blacks ever
known freedom in this Babylon?

HARRISON: I'm Harrison, Harrison Just, District
Attorney and you are?

CAPITÁN: Didn't ask your name, Suit and Tie, don't
need it. Sure, as hell, ain't giving ya mine.
What ya doing here?

HARRISON: You wouldn't happen to have any
information regarding the evening of Jaxson Price's
death?

CAPITÁN: They hung that boy-king like they did Jesus.
Lawd, how wicked them peoples' souls gotta be to do
a child in that way? Ya know me seen that boy king's
mother the day after they place him in that hollowed
earth. Her eyes. Me never seen that kind of sorrow in
a woman's eyes like that before. Like all the tears in
her body been poured out. Them eyes haunt me even
today.

HARRISON: What I'm asking is did you know him? Could you provide any information that might be of use to the investigation?

CAPITÁN: Investigation? No, no can't tell ya a thing. Didn't need to know the boy king to mourn him.

(CAPITÁN *walks away and leaves* HARRISON *by the swings alone.* HARRISON *approaches the swings. Touches it and the sound of windchimes can be hear. He pulls his hand away and it stops.)*

(Lights fade on LIL J, *and focus on* HARRISON *in his office with* LIL J's MOMMA....)

HARRISON: Thank you for coming, Ms Price.
Please have a seat... Please.

MOMMA: I guess I should say thank you for seeing me, Mr Harrison.

HARRISON: Of course. Please have a seat, ma'am. Would you like some coffee, or a coke? Danish maybe? Anything you'd like.

MOMMA: A glass of water would be nice.

HARRISON: Of course. Would you like anything with your water?

MOMMA: Straight. Just straight water.

HARRISON: You're sure? It's hot out there.

MOMMA: No water, I'm fine. I don't need any water. I can't be staying out too long. Like to be home before it starts getting dark if you don't mind.

HARRISON: It's so hot out there...weatherman said it's ninety or something crazy like that... It's no trouble at all.
I'm at your service.

MOMMA: I'm fine.
Fine.

(She looks out the window.)

Can you… Can you hear them out there? God, that crowd. Look at them. Standing out there under that hot sun… All them voices crying out in anger over my son. My baby. Seems unbelievable to me. Such a strange world we live in ain't it?

HARRISON: I'm sure it's difficult losing a son.

MOMMA: Mr Harrison. I buried my son three days ago, but I lost my son long before some dirty cops put their hands on him. I lost him when cops took…tragedies so many damn tragedies…tragedy followed that boy… Don't matter now.

He's gone. He's at peace, so I guess that's all that matters, I suppose. Look Mr Harrison, violence and loss been circling him long before any child should ever know what those things are… Like vultures feeding off his sorrow.

HARRISON: I know this might be difficult for you, ma'am, but can you talk to me a little bit about your son and his mental illness?

MOMMA: Why? So, you can go out there and protect those men that took my son from me?

HARRISON: I can say with absolute sincerity that the job of this office is to seek justice, not convictions… if evidence shows those men are guilty, no one in this office has any intention of protecting anyone that was involved with your son's death. We just need to know the details so that we can make sure everything is covered.

MOMMA: IF? If? You mean, they gonna slander my baby's name.

HARRISON: If we don't find out about it and get ahead of it then the defense will then, and yes, they will drag him through the dirt. And they'll love every minute of it. So please talk to me.

MOMMA: He was special... He could... He could see things. He could see things that others couldn't.

HARRISON: What do you mean see things?

MOMMA: Boy had seen so much tragedy in his life, eventually he could just see it everywhere he went. The pain he felt... Those cops who killed my boy they ended that pain. Ended one pain and sparked another.

HARRISON: Ma'am we have no proof as of this moment of murder, right now we just have questions...that need to be sorted through before we get to the right answer. But I want you to know that this office is doing everything in its power to get justice. We're here to help you.

MOMMA: Is that what you plan on doing?

HARRISON: We're going to do everything we can.

MOMMA: Oh...I see.

HARRISON: I don't understand.

MOMMA: You one of them kinda coons, ain't ya?

HARRISON: I beg your pardon.

MOMMA: I said you one of them kinda—

HARRISON: I heard what you said, ma'am...I assure you, we're on the same side.

MOMMA: ...

HARRISON: Ma'am...

MOMMA: You got questions? I got questions too. And my main question is are you going to do your damn job and bring whoever is responsible for killing my boy to justice?

HARRISON: I understand that you are hurt about losing your son.

MOMMA: Do you? Do you really?

HARRISON: I'll bring justice for your son. I'll do everything that I can to get him justice.

(MOMMA begins to cry. HARRISON pulls out a handkerchief and places it into her hand.

MOMMA: He wasn't just my son, my whole world orbited around that boy. He was my earth. You going to bring my world back? Cause right now, look at me I'm just spinning off course.
I'm not going to try and take up too much of your time. I know to you probably he was just a nobody. Just another young nigga dead on the street that you need to do paperwork on. Just another nigga that would have taken up some tax payer dollars… But he was my son.
I know you a busy man, but I want you to make me a promise.

HARRISON: I'm listening.

MOMMA: I want you to throw the man that killed my son into the deepest darkest pit of hell you can find… I want that murderer to spin into the same kind of darkness that he sent me when he killed my son. You hear me? Will you do that? Can you promise me that? Whoever did this to my boy I want you to make them pay.

HARRISON: I will do everything I can to find justice for this city and…your family.

MOMMA: I want you to promise.

(The shadowy figure of LIL J stands there in the darkness reaching out towards HARRISON. His hands are joined by

*others, they grab at him, lift him upwards and swallow him
into the darkness.)*

MOMMA: My son is calling for justice.
His voice can't be heard, so I need you to promise that
you'll speak for him.

(Lights swirl.)

(Lights swirl. MAYOR's office.)

MAYOR: First, I want to say this is a devastating event
that has taken place in the 4th Ward and within
the City of Houston. We are encouraging a full
investigation into the events that have taken place. We
hope that it is resolved as quickly as possible and we
are offering our condolences to the family of Jaxson
Price, to the citizens of this city, and we're working
to create policies in place to let the citizens of this city
know that Houston cares.

*(Sirens blare. A billboard reads "Houston Cares" shows
from above. Three protestors gather they hoist one of the
members of the group on their shoulders and they tag the
sign, so it reads "Houston Don't Care". They admire their
handy work once finished and then make a run for it.)*

*(The sound of hip hop and a growing roaring crowd. The
light shift and rises on the MAYOR, she is eating cake.
HARRISON enters.)*

MAYOR: Come in. Come in. How are you doing? Me
I didn't sleep at all last night. You know why? C N
N, Fox, *New York Times, U S A Today,* the *Sentinel,*
The Guardian and the *Tribune.* The media has been
hammering me lately. On top of that. I've been getting
calls all hours of the night from the Black Caucus,
the Urban League, N A A C P, the B E T, I swear if
they got black people somewhere in the name of their
organization I've gotten a call from them…Jesus, I've
never been so damn stress. All they want to talk about

Freedom Park. They want me to give up the officers'
names to the press. I thought you were handling this!
(She pauses.)
Ah, where's my manners... Would you like some cake?

HARRISON: No... No, I'm fine thank you.

MAYOR: More for me.
Harrison, let me ask you something.

HARRISON: Yeah sure go for it.

MAYOR: Haven't I been good to you? Haven't I been a
kind and benevolent soul? Generous to fault with you
and your department? Have I not?

HARRISON: You have.

MAYOR: Then why? Why you trying to ruin my life?
Why is my heart pressure up?

HARRISON: My guess would be because you're stress-
eating pastries.

MAYOR: Ha Ha...not the time for jokes.
I want this over with. I want this over with now, you
hear me.

HARRISON: I hear you. But to be fair only a day has
past.

MAYOR: Where are we at with this case?

HARRISON: It's not pretty. Heller's not talking, and we
aren't making any real leeway with anyone that we've
questioned thus far. We're doing what we can.

MAYOR: The clock is ticking. Get Heller talking.

HARRISON: I don't really know what you want me to
do?

MAYOR: You want to stay district attorney?
Then wake up. It's simple. Wrap this thing up.

HARRISON: It's not that simple. I have to find answers.

MAYOR: Answers. Think about this. Do you know the kind of hell on earth you'll bring down on our heads, if one of our law enforcement officers is found guilty of lynching a black kid?
Lynching! That would be the full weight of every damn police murder that ever happened thrown at us. We can't afford that right now. Not when I'm working so damn hard to transform 4th Ward into the Heights. Serious redevelopment funds are on the line here. We need this cleared up.

HARRISON: You act like I'm not.

MAYOR: Well it doesn't appear that way. It looks like you're dragging your goddamn feet. Just a few days, that's all we have…I got every black citizen and every black interest group calling for my head on a pike, I got people out on the streets screaming black lives matter. Wrap this thing up. I'm under siege here. You got me hanging by my nuts. By my fuckin' nuts!

HARRISON: Technically, Madame Mayor, you don't have any (*nuts*)—

MAYOR: Shut up, Harrison! You know what I mean. If this doesn't get resolved soon this city is about to be burn down! And I'm not going to have Fox News, charge me up saying this would never happen if the mayor was white! Or a man! So, do your job!

HARRISON: I'm trying to do my job.

MAYOR: Spare me.

I want this open and shut, like a cheap date!

HARRISON: Open and shut? It hasn't even been forty-eight hours yet. You want me to pull a miracle out of my ass?

MAYOR: Do your job or else.

(*Lights swirl and shift.* HARRISON *stands alone.*)

HARRISON: My grandpa once said that Houston is
where the devil goes for vacation. A city built on a
swamp. It's like a cruel punishment of throwing a
man into an oven and telling him to enjoy living there.
There's a heat to this place that seeps into your pores,
buries itself deep into your skin, and then roasts and
boils your soul…and left unchecked. If not allowed
to cool it boils out into the streets and turns into rage.
That's what was happening in the streets of 4th Ward,
Houston, Texas.

(The sound of cameras snapping.)

(The sound of protestors.)

*(A PROTESTER stands in a Black Lives Matter T-shirt
speaking into a bullhorn.)*

PROTESTER: You want to know the truth about the pig
department? You want to know the truth about them
that nobody is willing to say? The P-I-G Department
has no obligation to help you. It's not the job of the
State to protect the public, the American judicial
system put that in place. Making it so the only job the
police really must do is maintain order and enforce the
law. Maintain order. Maintain order… Think about
what that means brothas and sistas. One got to ask
whose order?
They are only servants to the state, they are not here
to serve the people. Their job is not to protect you, it's
to arrest you, fill the city's treasury with your dollars
spent paying fines and court fees, and maintain the
status quo… Especially if you're Black.
Blacks jailed five times more than whites. Oh no!!!
Don't believe the lies. It's not because Blacks commit
more crimes, that's a racially biased statistic, it's
because this country was founded by white people…
I'm going to say it, I'm going to say it… for white

people but built with the blood and sweat from our ancestors. But you not ready to hear that truth. These cops don't serve to protect, they serve to kill and walk out of a courtroom with a smile on their face. That's the truth this city hall doesn't want you to know. To serve and protect is just a catchphrase. Made up by the police to fool the people. Wake up! Wake up! Wake up!

(Lights shift and swirl.)

(Police Office)

HELLER: Ah, hell what are you doing here? I got to clock in to shift. They have me working motor pool till they figure out what to do with me.

I can't be late.

HARRISON: I spoke with the chief, he agreed to our meeting. Glad to see you out your cell.

HELLER: Yeah, well I'm glad to be out. What do you want man?

HARRISON: The mayor wants us to bring your case before a grand jury.

HELLER: Is that good?

HARRISON: Trial ends either one of two ways... I feel like we shouldn't have this conversation without an attorney present for you.

HELLER: I'm going to be my own attorney.

HARRISON: I don't think that's wise.

HELLER: I'm not one that is concerned about what's wise or not. I'm doing what I think is right.

HARRISON: Officer Heller.

HELLER: Look you...you get to go home at the end of the day. Sit at home. Watch T V, eat a home cooked dinner, maybe lay up next to some pretty wife and close your eyes to a beautiful world out there.

But me...

Yeah, I don't get that. I've got this thing hanging over me. On top of that I got half my pay docked, I slept in a jail cell, and everyday I'm scared to leave the house cause I'm thinking any minute now, the news is going to leak my name.

And I haven't done a damn thing wrong.

Didn't do a damn thing wrong except wearing this uniform of blue when some street trash took himself out. I don't deserve this.

HARRISON: Street trash?

HELLER: Look a kid lost his life. It's a tragedy. And I feel terrible about that, but I didn't have nothing to do with his death.

HARRISON: Good, then you won't have any problem telling me about what happened that night? That night of Jaxson's death?

HELLER: I don't recall...

HARRISON: But that night wasn't the first time you had encountered Mr Price?

HELLER: No—

HARRISON: Officer Heller, do you recall any of our past conversations?

HELLER: A little. Why?

HARRISON: (*Opens his briefcase, pulls out a stack of files*) You told me that you didn't know him.

HELLER: What...what...what are you getting at?

HARRISON: Did you know him or not?

HELLER: Yeah, I mean, he was just a kid on my beat.

HARRISON: But you had multiple encounters with him. Much more than four or five…

HELLER: Yeah but—

HARRISON: So, you knew him.

HELLER: You're twisting up my words?

HARRISON: Is that what I'm doing?

HELLER: What do you want from me?

HARRISON: Just the truth. Are you willing to tell me the truth, so we can proceed with things?
Yes or no? Officer Heller, I'm trying to be on your side here.
You know it's not too late to get someone…a lawyer…a union rep…

HELLER: No!!!
I'll…I'm…I'm going to represent myself. I didn't hang that kid.

HARRISON: So, you are prepared to talk to me? Honestly?

HELLER: Yeah, I'll tell you whatever I can.

HARRISON: Good… Can you tell me about how you first came to encounter Mr Price?

HELLER: Me and my partner officer Tomms found him trespassing in a park at night. We approached him to have a conversation, and politely asked him to relocate elsewhere.

HARRISON: And that wasn't the last time that you had encountered Mr Price.

HELLER: No, no it wasn't…

HARRISON: Can you give us a brief summary of your other encounters before the night of his death?

HELLER: Yeah, we'd be on patrol and he'd always be at that park, you know. Always there. No matter how many times we told him to go, we'd always found him there. We convinced him a few times to relocate, after a point we'd escort him to his mother's house. Eventually we had to arrest him a few times, throw him in a cell... But I didn't kill him.

HARRISON: You put a minor in a jail cell with adults?

HELLER: Figured it was better than us calling CPS on him. We hoped a night in a cell, he'd get the drift.

HARRISON: Tell me about your experiences with him.

(LIL J *appears onstage.*)

HARRISON: Walk me through the fourth encounter that you had with him.

HELLER: Why? Why the fourth one...

HARRISON: Just trying to make sense of this note... It looks pretty straight forward in the report but then there is this one notation in the corner that says simply...mayo. Help me make sense of this.

(HELLER *rises from his feet and walks toward* LIL J.)

HELLER: I was on my beat, and I decide I'm going to circle around and I see standing at the playground that kid...that kid. Just standing there and talking to someone in the darkness...

HARRISON: He was talking to someone?

HELLER: I don't know... Maybe himself...I don't honestly don't know. It was after hours and... So, I go up to him. I had to do my job.
(*To* LIL J)
Hey, hey kid.
Hey kid, thought we told you can't be out here after hours.

LIL J: What you bugging me for man? Ain't you got some drug dealers or some shit to be chasin'?

HELLER: You know I got to do my job, kid.

LIL J: Well do your job somewhere else? I ain't hurting nobody.

HELLER: Doesn't matter kid, its trespassing and it's unlawful for any minor under 17 to be on public property between the hours of 11pm to 6am without parental supervision. You, young man are violating not one but two laws.

LIL J: I guess I'm a rebel like that.

HELLER: I guess you are, kid.

HARRISON: Where was Tomms?

LIL J: Where's your friend?

HELLER: The kid's not violent so I told Tomms to wait in the car.

HARRISON: Why did you do that?

HELLER: Tomms has a tendency not to play well with his own people if you know what I mean.

HARRISON: Alright continue.

LIL J: Ah gotcha. That makes sense.

HELLER: You can't be out here. Head home.

LIL J: This is my home.

HELLER: No kid, home like to your mom and dad.

LIL J: Why you keep calling me kid, man? Like I'm some kinda baby sheep you about to sacrifice or some shit.

HELLER: Goat.

LIL J: That's even worse.

HELLER: Kid… Look…I don't think of you as some goat to be sacrificed,
I'm just trying to help keep you out of trouble these streets are dangerous at night. Especially in the park. Nothing but dope fiends and bangers hang out in the park after hours.

LIL J: I'm not a banger or a fiend and I'm up in the park. Freedom Park is supposed to be for the people.

HELLER: Well you maybe the rare exception to the rule, but the majority out in the parks during these hours is out looking for trouble. You don't want to get involved into the kind of trouble like what's out here.
What is your name? You mind telling me your name?

LIL J: It's Jaxson.

HELLER: Alright Jaxson. Jaxson…Jaxson what?

LIL J: Price.

HELLER: Look you're a minor, and we can't have you out here alone at night. Let me take you home. Can I do that?
(*To* HARRISON)
After that he complied. Put him in the back of the squad car and took him to his mother's. Had to do that repeatedly. Every night the same thing. Jaxson would be standing out there talking to someone, to himself, to the shadows, who the hell knows, I'd approach him. Give him the same speech over and over again and then put him in the squad car, take him home. Tomms was starting to get aggravated, Hell, I was starting to get annoyed having to put it in my reports every night. But we didn't kill him. I didn't kill him. I liked him. Hell, I even once…
(*To* LIL J)
You want a sandwich, kid?

LIL J: There you go with that sacrificial baby goat stuff. You planning on sacrificing' me to your evil god of corruption and greed?

HELLER: Do you want a sandwich or not, Jaxson?

LIL J: Maybe, what type?

HELLER: Pastrami, ham and cheese. I'll give you half of mine.

LIL J: It got mayo in it? I know you white people love mayo.

HELLER: Well you're in luck it's got mayo. Living up to the stereotype.

LIL J: I'll take half.

HELLER: Well you were only gonna get half.

LIL J: This some kind of bribe or something?

HELLER: Can't get nothing by you huh, kid?

LIL J: About time you figure that out.

Hands Lil J part of his sandwich.

HELLER: Look my partner is getting pissed. You can't keep coming out here after hours and breaking curfew.

LIL J: Man, I gotta. This the only time my girl can come see me.

HELLER: Well you going to have to find another place to meet up with her. I don't know maybe before curfew. Have you considered that? Where is this chick anyway?

LIL J: She around, she just doesn't like cops, had a bad experience once with them, so she keeps her distance.

HELLER: She must be amazing you risking it to meet her all the time like this.

LIL J: Ah man. She's…she's amazing. Shorty is impressive. She's an honor student, and does spoken word art. She's hella smart.

HELLER: Alright, alright… well, hey, Jaxson look. My partner said that if we catch you here again we're going to have to bring you in for trespassing. You got to pass that message on to your girlfriend as well, alright? You got me?

LIL J: Yeah, I hear you.

HELLER: So, we not gonna see you around here no more, right?

LIL J: Saying yes, the only way you gonna leave me alone, huh?

HELLER: I'm still gonna have to take you home.

LIL J: Man, really?

HELLER: Yeah, man really? Come on, let's go.

(Lights swirl.)

(The MAYOR *stands at a pedestal for a press conference.)*

MAYOR: At this time while we grieve for the mother of Jaxson Price. We can not say that it was a city of Houston police officer who caused that young man's death. In fact, we feel that making any such accusation against the police that protect and serve this city at this time is speculative, dangerous, and ultimately un-American. We however will be launching a full investigation with our extremely capable District Attorney Harrison Just leading the charge and we can assure you that justice will be swift and harsh on those who committed this heinous crime. Thank you, for your time, Houston Cares!

(Light shift.)

HARRISON: That night as I laid by my wife. Hand resting on her swollen belly, I had a strange dream.

I saw the boy standing in the darkness, looking out towards me.

He stretches out his arm towards me, like he was pleading for me to help him… His mouth open screaming for me but no words came out… Begging for me to save him…I woke up that night covered in my own cold sweat, drenched.

(Lights shift and swirl. HARRISON, *the* MAYOR, *and* MOMMA.*)*

MAYOR: Ma'am, we just wanted to let you know that we are doing everything in our power to make things right.

MOMMA: You gonna bring my son back from the dead like Lazarus? Cause right now that's the only damn way I see you can make things right.

MAYOR: This isn't easy for any of us.

MOMMA: You sure about that mayor? My boy died in May… It's July and all I'm seeing is you and Mr Just over there sitting in your cushy offices. Reading in the paper about you all going out having your fancy happy hours and five hundred dollars a plate donor-dinners, but the rest of us are living in the real world!

MAYOR: Ms Price!

HARRISON: We're doing what we can. We've begun questioning and combing through the information. Progress is slow but believe us when we say it's coming.

How long! How long am I supposed to wait for justice? A day? Months? Years? Decades? You tell me that!

MAYOR: Ms Price, I can assure you that police violence has no place in this community. It will not be tolerated and we're going to do what we can to get to the bottom of this. That much I can promise you.

MOMMA: You made a lot of promises. I ain't see you do none of them yet... You just like every other politician ain't you? To think I voted for you.

MAYOR: Like I said we're doing everything we can to fix this issue, to defuse the situation. We're not the enemy here.

MOMMA: Are you?

MAYOR: In the meantime, we need your help.

MOMMA: Oh, that's funny. You want my help?

HARRISON: We do. Two things really.

MOMMA: What you want?

MAYOR: Houston has had many storms, ones that have torn this city apart. But we always rebuild. I'm worried this city can't survive this kind of storm. We need to calm the storm before it grows into something that we can't stop.

We're going to get to the bottom of this. We need you to go out there and speak to the community. Tell them that there needs to be order to things... That there is a process in place to put wrongs right. Can you do that? Can you do that for us? For this city? Can you quiet the storm? Bring a little kumbi-yah moment to the city.

MOMMA: And the other thing?

HARRISON: Ms Price, our reports show that he was estranged from your home. That he was picked up by the police multiple times for delinquency and truancy, and trespassing can you tell us about your relationship with your son?

MOMMA: What does that have to do with anything?

HARRISON: It will merely help us get a full picture of everything as we piece this all together.

MOMMA: He was a free spirit that's all it was. Don't mean nothing. Don't mean he was a bad child. I tried to get that boy to come home. Tried everyway I could.

(Lights shift and swirl. The sound of the streets. A siren goes by.)

(Lights comes up on LIL J *sitting on the playground. He counts a wad of cash and carefully tucks it away into his hiding place. It isn't long before he realizes someone is behind him.)*

MOMMA: Jaxson.

LIL J: Hey Mama. What you doing here? It's starting to get dark.

MOMMA: I could ask you the same thing. You know the night ain't kind to us.

LIL J: I ain't worried.

MOMMA: Anyhow I ain't gonna be stayin' out here too long.
I bought you some dinner, figured you must be hungry being here like this.
All your favorite in here. Little bit of catfish, green beans, mash potato.
You hungry, aren't you?

*(*LIL J *takes the food. He sits and begins to eat.)*

*(*MOMMA *moves towards him. Touches his head lovingly. Tender)*

LIL J: Thank you, momma.

MOMMA: You been takin' your—

LIL J: You already know the answer.

MOMMA: They supposed to help you.

LIL J: Well they don't. Fog my head up. Can't see things straight like I need to… Don't need that. What else you doin' here momma?

MOMMA: You plan on coming home anytime soon?

(LIL J *pulls away.*)

LIL J: I'm cool, momma. I can't be staying over there no more ma. The bed so small my feet dangle off the damn thing. And I don't get to see…I wouldn't get to see her, if I stay over there.

MOMMA: She means that much to you?

LIL J: I'm good, momma. Don't be worrying about me.

MOMMA: I'm your momma, Jaxson, it's my job to worry. And I know…it's hard you being all grown up and all but you still my son. Come back home. Come stay with us. Have a hot meal. A hot bath. Be somewhere other than out in these streets. You know I be worrying about you. Come home and surround your life with people who love you.

LIL J: You need go home, mama.

MOMMA: Don't be tellin' me what I need to be doin'. I'm a mother. I need to take care of you. Come home to me, Jaxson. You think I don't know what you be doin'. You keep running these streets—

LIL J: I'm not slangin' mama. I'm hustling D V Ds and shit.

MOMMA: It's still illegal.

LIL J: Sometimes you got to do a little wrong to make your world right. That's all I'm doing in this life.

MOMMA: Hustling' is still hustlin', Jaxson. You can't keep this up.

LIL J: Momma stop it.

MOMMA: Alright, I'm done talkin'. Don't have to hear my mouth no more.

LIL J: Thank you. You need to get home. You not looking so good.

(Silence)

MOMMA: People don't know history no more. Don't appreciate it. You know this park.

Use to be where Clarence and Sadie May Jenkins use to live here before old man Clarence burned it down, then it became the spot where all the kids use to come gather after school, kissed your daddy Allah for the first time right by them swings, right there.

Funny no matter whether it was the backyard of the Jenkins family, or the place we'd play hide and seek, tag, or kiss the girl, it was always the place where the youth could feel safe to gather. Place where it was okay for black kids to get to be kids. Now look at it. Look at that these people have let this place turn into.

Nothing but rusty reminders of joys long forgotten. Just a place where restless spirits walk amongst us. I don't want that for you. I don't want to see you turn into one of these ghosts walkin' amongst us. Come back home. Come back to your momma. A mother's job is simple. Give you a sense of self. Give them a little bit of pride in themselves to carry with them as a shield against a world that just wants to tear them asunder. But most of all its to love and protect their child. There's so many things out here wanting to rip a Black boy apart and I can't...I can't protect you out here. Come home.

(The lights swirl and shift. REVEREND, *the* MAYOR, *and* HARRISON. *The* MAYOR *is eating pudding.)*

REVEREND: You couldn't have the code of silence here if the higher-up police officials, the state's attorney, and assistant state's attorneys, and the judges all didn't work together for this to keep going.

MAYOR: I assure you, Reverend McHenry we are doing everything we can.

REVEREND: Bet you say that quite often, Madam Mayor. Why do I struggle to believe that?

MAYOR: We have District Attorney Just handling this personally. You know D A Just right?

REVEREND: I do. How's your wife? Little one on the way, right? Congrats.

HARRISON: Thank you, she's doing good, Reverend.

REVEREND: Good. Well I'm hoping to see you in service this Sunday. It's been awhile.

HARRISON: We'll do our best.

MAYOR: Speaking of doing our best… Reverend, the city is doing everything we can to make sure all parties are being heard.

REVEREND: Kind of hard to be heard when you are buried in the grave.

MAYOR: McHenry… Listen.

REVEREND: No… You've got your spin doctors all over this.

MAYOR: Reverend we are containing the crisis—

REVEREND: Let me finish…Jaxson before he went downhill was an honor roll student, volunteered at the old folks' home, was a brilliant artist. His mother attends our church regularly, but you made it so that the media drags that boys name through the damn dirt. You don't share that with the media now did ya? What does him not being on the medication prescribed to him have to do with his murder?

MAYOR: Reverend it has everything to do with this case. We're trying to clear it up the best we can.

REVEREND: Doesn't look like it to me.

MAYOR: Well I beg your pardon but what does it look like to you?

REVEREND: With all due respect it looks like you are sitting on your ass over here. That's what it looks like to me. This isn't the first time this city has tried this mess.
(Picks up a file from a purse and slams it down on the desk.)

MAYOR: Jesus

REVEREND: 2010, Officers Martinez guns down Greg Brown, claiming he opened fire on them. No gun at the scene.
(Pulls out other slams it to the desk.)
The murder of Clay Damiano in 2002, Officers in the shooting Rick Lyons and Tyler Austin found a gun but did not find any fingerprints on it, one witness to Damiano shooting, said in a police statement that he saw a gun in Johnson's hand. Now after Austin retired that witnessed claimed that he didn't see Damiano holding a gun and that officers threatened him with a charge if he didn't go along with their story.
(Pulls out another file slams it to the desk.)
Domestic Dispute 2012 between a mother and a son... Officer Clemens arrives, and he guns down a twenty year-old kid for supposedly charging him, shooting him thirteen times. Then supposedly according to the mother stands over him and shoots him three more times. Clemens is given desk duty for a month and then cleared.
(Pulls out another file and slams it down.)
We all know the Eric Strong story. Don't we, mayor?

MAYOR: You can't put that death on this administration!!

REVEREND: Oh, but we can put on this city.
(Pulls out more files and slams them to the desk.)
Seventy-five year-old lady slammed to the concrete with a boot pressed down on her head.

A former marine randomly stopped and had five guns drawn on him for jaywalking.

A twelve-year-old boy thrown in the back of a police car cause his bike didn't have brakes, and he accidentally crashed into it.

Off duty police officer shoots two brothers in the parking lot of a bar over a girl. Evidence later shows he was drunk at the time.

Seven-year-old shot dead for having a toy gun. Honor roll student shot in his own driveway.

There's plenty more reports as well. Just like these. Each time their stories get ignored, and time after time your police seem to be protected. When is enough going to be enough?

HARRISON: I assure you that this investigation is being thorough.

REVEREND: I don't want you to assure me the investigation is thorough. All those cases where black and brown bodies find themselves on blood stained floors those investigations were thorough.

HARRISON: Then what do you want from us?

REVEREND: I want you to look me the eyes and tell me that you know that in your heart "Black lives do matter!" That's what I want. We have bullies and killers out on these streets and we aren't talking about the gangsters and the thugs. No, the community put you in office. If you can't do your jobs, then we'll put someone else in that will. You hold on to these reports Mr Just. There's one other name in these files that you might find an interest in. Think you'll find the name of the Officer connected to each and every single one of these atrocities will sound familiar to you?

(Lights shift and swirl. Freedom Park. DAEJAH *and* LIL J*)*

DAEJAH: What's up?

LIL J: Why you always got to sneak up on me like that?

DAEJAH: Man, I don't know how you keep coming over here? Especially after everything that went down with...I just don't get it.

LIL J: This is Freedom Park, girl! Where else would I be? You here.

DAEJAH: That don't mean nothin'. I ain't nobody.

LIL J: You are to me.

DAEJAH: You need to quit coming around here. It ain't safe. Not ever soul here is down for you like that.

LIL J: Look here's my thinkin'. As long as you going to meet me here, I'm going to show up.

DAEJAH: Then maybe I should stop showing up. Maybe I ought to go talk to your momma, see if she'll talk some sense into you.

LIL J: Stay away from my momma. She doesn't need weight on her soul like that.

DAEJAH: I'm just sayin'.

LIL J: Stay away from my momma! What's between us is between us.

DAEJAH: She worried about you man. Hell, we all worried about you.

LIL J: Well, as you can see I'm fine.

DAEJAH: Aight.

LIL J: Aight. Fine.

DAEJAH: Fine.

LIL J: —

New subject. New topic let's flip this mood.

DAEJAH: Alright, what you want to talk about.

LIL J: —

Loving you.

DAEJAH: Nah, don't be tryin' to kiss me, after you've been getting' an attitude with me and everything.

LIL J: C'mon now, we moved on to new topic. Give me a kiss.

DAEJAH: Boy, you stupid.

LIL J: But you like it though.

(DAEJAH *and* LIL J *kiss.*)

LIL J: Oh, hey check it out.

(LIL J *goes to his money stash and* DAEJAH *follows.*)

LIL J: This stack keeps rising. One more month and we get the hell on out of here. Together.

DAEJAH: You know we can't.

LIL J: We can. We will.

(*Police siren*)

(DAEJAH *scrambles. Motions for* LIL J *to follow*)

DAEJAH: J!!! J come on!!!

(LIL J *hides his money away and turns to follow* DAEJAH *as she fades into the darkness.*)

(TOMMS *appears onstage.*)

TOMMS: Hey, hey, Stop right there.

LIL J: Ah shit.

TOMMS: (*To* LIL J) Who's your friend? Where are they hiding?

LIL J: Nobody. Nobody but me and you.

TOMMS: Cute.

LIL J: What? You think I'm cute…that's like the nicest thing you've ever said.

I must be growing on ya.

(LIL J *and* TOMMS *laugh but are silenced when* TOMMS *punches* LIL J.)

TOMMS: Yeah, you growin' on me. You growin' on me like cancer on an ass cheek.

LIL J: What the hell man? What the hell?!!! Hey man, that wasn't called for! You can't be doing that we got rights and shit.

(He gets to his feet and tries to leave.)

TOMMS: Where you think you're going?

LIL J: Man, I'm going home. You win alright. Message loud and clear. What do you want from me?

TOMMS: I said stop right there!

LIL J: Why you gotta be messing with me all the time.

TOMMS: Messing with you? I'm messing with you? Is that what I'm doing?

LIL J: I'm not scared of you.

TOMMS: Oh, but you should be. I'm the boogie man to little punk boys like you. And your friend Heller ain't here to hand out turkey sandwiches. So it's me and you today, kid.

LIL J: It was pastrami.

TOMMS: Shut up kid.

LIL J: Look man, I'm going home, okay. I'm going home.

TOMMS: And I said you stay.
Good boy.
Why you lookin' at me like that? You got a problem?

LIL J: Nah.

TOMMS: You keep trying to make eye contact with me. Seems like you must have a problem with me.

LIL J: Man—

TOMMS: Don't "Man" me, you see me, you say sir. In fact, you don't even look at me...
You understand that?
I asked if you understand me, boy?

LIL J: Yes...

TOMMS: Yes what?

LIL J: Yes sir.

TOMMS: Good boy. There you go with that eye contact thing you keep doing?
You trying to stare me down or something?

LIL J: Just realizing what a real monster looks like...sir.

TOMMS: Get out of here, before I show you what a real monster looks like. And I swear to God, if I see you trespassing at this park again? If I have to jam another pencil into a sharpener again because of you or write your little ghetto ass name on a report one more damn time I'll beat the ever-loving shit out of you. Get out of here and don't let me see you again you fuckin'—

(LIL J *punches* TOMMS. *Black out*)

(HARRISON *and* TOMMS *stare each other down* HARRISON *sitting and* TOMMS *standing in front of the interrogation room table.*)

HARRISON: Hello Officer Tomms—

TOMMS: Sergeant.

HARRISON: I'm sorry Sergeant Tomms. I'm—

TOMMS: I know who you are.

HARRISON: Is that so?

TOMMS: You must be so damn proud of yourself. Letting a good cop go through the ringer like this.

HARRISON: Is he?

TOMMS: What?

HARRISON: A good cop? For that matter, are you?

TOMMS: Fuck you.

HARRISON: Sir. You must have me confused...
If I take off this tie we're going to have a completely
different kind of conversation. You understand me.
You don't have to like me, but you will answer my
questions.
Now why don't you have a seat.

TOMMS: I'd rather stand.

HARRISON: And I said... Take. A. Seat.

(TOMMS *sits.*)

HARRISON: Now, where were you the night in question
of Jaxson Price's death?

TOMMS: No comment.

HARRISON: The night in question did you or Heller,
radio in that you were about to question Jaxson Price?

TOMMS: No comment.

HARRISON: Did you or your partner call at all for backup?

TOMMS: No comment.

HARRISON: Let record show that on the date of the
event there was no call whatsoever that came from
their car.
(*To* TOMMS)
God, you must feel so proud of your damn self.

TOMMS: No. Comment. How many more times you
need me to say it?

HARRISON: We're playing this, are we?
Let's try this one again. How would you describe
Officer Heller?

TOMMS: He's a good cop.

HARRISON: And what was your opinion of Jaxson Price?

TOMMS: He was just a kid

HARRISON: And did you stance regarding that kid change in any way?

TOMMS: What do you mean?

HARRISON: I mean you're a big man, Tomms, you must have felt like quite a punk when that kid whooped you.

TOMMS: What are you talkin' about?

HARRISON: Eye witness reports came in said you tried to rough him up and he dropped you hard. Says you decide to rough him up again as usual and you got floored. What happened huh? Ego get bruised along with that eye. Is that why you and Heller killed that boy.

TOMMS: Hey, the kid sucker punched me, but we didn't kill nobody.

HARRISON: What happened to no comment?

TOMMS: Look I had nothing to do with what happened. Did me and my partner, have a problem with the little shit kid? Yeah sure...I mean if something bad happened to the kid, good fuckin' riddance but it wasn't me and it damn sure wasn't my partner who strung that kid up... We didn't do that. So, don't put that on me.

HARRISON: So, then what you did you do to him?

TOMMS: Don't go trying to put words in my mouth, we followed procedure. We do good police work—

HARRISON: At all times?

TOMMS: Yeah at all time!

HARRISON: So this flask doesn't belong to you then?

(He reveals a flask.)

TOMMS: Where'd you get that?

HARRISON: Believe it or not your squad car. This is your's right?

TOMMS: Nah, must be somebody else's

HARRISON: There's someone else that drives your squad car that would have engraved your exact same name on it? What are the odds?

TOMMS: I know what your fucking doing?

HARRISON: You see, anything that could help us out here. We're just trying to—

TOMMS: Take down a cop. A good cop. And your hoping to use me as your puppet. Yeah, I know. You know what? I grew up in that neighborhood. Spent my life growing up amongst them people.
Right there in the heart of 4th Ward, my own mom's house was right by that park that boy died in. Watched as that once beautiful black neighborhood twisted itself with drugs and violence. The things I have seen out there...day after day...the evil...the sick fuckin' horror that's out there. The things these people do to each other...I can't even call them my own anymore. The things...the things I've seen I tell you this much it would make angels weep, and believe me, oh how they've wept. And you paint the people who maintain that thin line between hell and civilization as the bad guys—

HARRISON: A kid is dead. A black kid. And I would think that as a—

TOMMS: All I see blue. That's the only color that I see. That's the only color that matters in my book. Don't see Black, don't see White... You put on the uniform. That's the only color that matters. Every day, we put our damn lives on the lines for you ingrates. We endure the pay freezes, and the budget redistributions, and most of us Heller included left warzones out in Afghanistan or Iraq, or whatever the hell else and get dropped right in the middle of the warzone of that is these streets and we do it together. United.

HARRISON: Wait, say that again.
Say that again that thing about being dropped into warzones.

TOMMS: What that got to do with anything.

HARRISON: Nothing, probably its nothing, just something you said connected for me. One last question for, Sgt Tomms...Tell me about a young woman you encountered a year ago named Daejah?

TOMMS: No... We're done. Next time you want to talk to me... You can talk to my fuckin' lawyer.

(Lights shift and swirl finding HARRISON *standing alone.)*

HARRISON: When I returned home that day, as I climbed up the steps, I tripped over an open bottle of malt liquor and when I look up, I found a dead rat hanging from a metal chain noose on my front door. The arms, legs, and neck entangled in them. The mouth of that rodent gaping wide open. Their message was clear.

(Lights swirl.)

(HARRISON *and* HELLER *in the interrogation room.)*

HELLER: Mr Just, you called me in? Can you make this quick? I'm supposed to report back to the desk in thirty.

(HARRISON *throws down a stack of files onto the table.)*

HARRISON: Twenty-five or six interactions with Jaxson Price within the duration of a year.

HELLER: Wait a minute.

HARRISON: You do realize that my job is to decide whether we charge you with this kid murder or, not right? And you're going to lie to me when your life is in the balance?

HELLER: I'm an officer of the law, you really think I'm capable of that?!!
This is crazy.

HARRISON: Is it? Is that what this is? Or is it me pointing out the fact that you had a hand in that kids' death?

HELLER: You know what?!! I'm done here. You have anything else to say to me talk to my attorney and my union rep.

HARRISON: Oh, now you decide you want a union rep. Let me tell you what happens once we call that union rep. We haven't charged you with anything. No one knows that you are here currently under investigation, we call that union rep.
Then we got to charge you. We must charge you. Once we charge you... Somehow or another your name gets leaked to the press. The community now knows that you are suspected of killing an unarmed kid. No not killing... Lynching. You think Ferguson was bad? You think Baltimore, Oakland, Saint Louis were bad? Those aren't going to touch what happens here. You become the poster child for every shitty murderous cop that ever killed a kid. Do you want that?

HELLER: No.

HARRISON: Is that what you want? Cause damnit it I'll happily oblige you!

HELLER: No!
(He gasps.)

HARRISON: Then I suggest, my friend, that you start talking.

HELLER: Alright we crossed paths a more than a couple of times. It's in the reports.

HARRISON: I know it's in there. But now you walk me through it. Walk me through the night of Jaxson Price's death.

HELLER: I told you everything I have to say.

HARRISON: Walk me through it, Heller, it doesn't make sense to me.

HELLER: I don't have anything to say.

HARRISON: Witnesses found you at the scene.

HELLER: …

HARRISON: Why didn't you call it in? So why didn't you follow procedure and call it in?
You saw the body. Dangling from the swing set. That boy was hanging from a swing set by his neck and there you were just staring up at him. Why didn't you call it in?
A teenage boy is found hanging and you figured, "Oh, well let me just sit here"

HELLER: I was freaking out, alright! I've seen gaping holes in people's bodies, I've seen bloody stubs from limbs blown off my friends, but I… But I haven't…I haven't ever seen anything like that before, you know?

HARRISON: Or maybe you just wanted to stare and admire your handiwork.

(*Light shift and swirl.* HARRISON *stands and speaks and as he speaks one by one shadowy figures appear behind him.*)

HARRISON: That night as I laid by my wife. Tossed and turned…Staring at the ceiling… Staring at her. Hand resting on her swollen belly, finally once I faded off to sleep that dream…that dream that comes back and haunts me night after night returns…I see Jaxson standing in the darkness, looking out to towards me.

He stretches out his arm towards me, like he was pleading for me to help him... Begging for me to save him... And then out of the darkness stepped one by one, thousands upon thousands of men and women and children. Some riddled with bullet holes, other necks stretched, hangmen nooses still wrapped around their necks.

Death upon each of their faces. All of them reaching out towards me. Their blood pours out from their bodies like a leak in a dam. Flows toward me like a wild river and drowns me. Drowning me in an ocean of their blood. Fighting my way to the top I gasp for breath and the screams of a thousand of dying voices roars from my lungs. I wake up covered in my own sweat, drenched. Only fifteen days left.

(Lights shift and swirl.)

NEWSCASTER 2: Good morning, today in news we've discovered that the police officer accused of the murder of black teen Jaxson Price has been placed on desk duty. More news to come.

(Lights shift and swirl. MOMMA *is in* HARRISON's *office.)*

MOMMA: They let him out? News is saying they got that officer on desk duty. Desk duty what is that?

HARRISON: I'm sorry. He's been on desk duty for about a month now. We should have told you.

MOMMA: So while my son is dead in the grave, that man gets to sit at his desk, playing tetris, and collecting a check?!! How's that justice?

HARRISON: We had no choice around that. Have a seat.

MOMMA: I'd rather stand.

HARRISON: Would you like some tea, coffee?

MOMMA: I'm fine.

HARRISON: Look I'm sorry to bring this up again but can you tell me about your son's mental illness?

MOMMA: He ain't had no mental illness, he was just someone that can see things that others can't.
His mind just worked different than most.

HARRISON: In the same way that your mind also works a little different.

MOMMA: How you know that?

HARRISON: The need to get home before dark, auditory and visual hallucinations, list is long. My investigations show that you take quite a few pills for your condition. Same medication that your son was supposed to take. Mild schizophrenia. Sees things that's not there?

MOMMA: It's not schizophrenia or whatever them silly doctors want to call it. We simply see the shadows. My family been able to do that since lord knows how long. That's all it is. What's that got to do with anything?

HARRISON: The defense is going to bring this up. In fact the state of his mental health has to be leaked to the press already.

MOMMA: You're going to let this man get off cause he's white and my son... my son is what? Just some kid on medication to you is that how it's going to be? Victimize and then villainize my child...my boy. I thought you were on my son's side. Were you lying to me? I just want my son's truth to be heard. Why is that so hard for you people to let happen without dirtying who he was?

(Lights take MOMMA *away.)*

(Lights shift and swirl.)

CORONER: Good Morning.

HARRISON: If you can call it that.

Said you had something you wanted to tell me about this case?

CORONER: I'm not sure…you want good news or the "what the fuck?" type of news?

HARRISON: Just give it to me.

CORONER: You're going to hate me.

HARRISON: I've always hated you. Spill it.

CORONER: Well you're going to hate me even more now. It appears you have two issues on your hand.

HARRISON: Two?

CORONER: A beating and rape, and then a suicide.

HARRISON: Rape? You said a rape?

CORONER: He was raped with a blunt object.

(CORONER *hands* HARRISON *a file.*)

HARRISON: They…they raped him? So, looking at this report what am I looking at here?
Help me make sense of this.

CORONER: Well from what we gathered he suffered multiple head trauma, then was raped with a blunt object before he was tied up. From what I'm seeing they beat him bad.

HARRISON: Any way to tell what it was?

CORONER: If I had to make a guess… Police baton. Jammed it right up his—

HARRISON: Why wasn't this in my coroner's report when I took the case?

CORONER: Police chief got it…
Mayor got it…
If I had to guess it's because nobody likes you.

HARRISON: Thanks.

CORONER: Just doing what I can.

HARRISON: So, what about the hanging? You said it
was a suicide. How can it be?

CORONER: Looks like after his assault he dragged
himself over to the swing set tied himself up and…
The marks around his wrists and neck suggest that he
strangled himself. Bruises on the wrist, bruises on the
neck. The hanging appears self-inflicted. I know that's
not what you wanted to hear.
His neck isn't broken. Looks like he was hanging there
for a good two hours before his life left him. Can you
imagine that? How many people must have passed by
his body just hanging there like that and didn't do a
thing about it…God, why is this city so evil?

HARRISON: Thanks that helps. I owe you coffee.

CORONER: You owe me lunch… Oh one more thing.

HARRISON: Yeah?

CORONER: I thought that the site of the investigation
was familiar. So, did some combing through my files
and…

HARRISON: And what?

CORONER: See for yourself.
History repeats itself.
History always repeats itself.

*(The CORONER hands HARRISON the file. He opens scans
through it and stops.)*

HARRISON: Holy shit.

CORONER: I told you that you'd be owing me lunch.

HARRISON: You keep this quiet. You don't let this leak
to no one. You hear me.
I don't want to hear that none of this leaked to the
news. Not this and not the rape.

CORONER: Won't be coming from out of my mouth that's for damn sure.

(Lights shift and swirl. HARRISON *standing alone)*

HARRISON: Who could be capable of doing something so…horrible to someone? Why would anyone do that to someone? I got off work and instead of driving home like usual…I walked. I walked long hard blocks home. Miles upon miles… From downtown city hall, pass court houses, passed luxury lofts and five-star restaurants, I walked past ram-shackled building and tenement blocks, I walked past burnt out buildings way past repair…I walked down the freeway all the way towards home…

Trying to push the thought of what that poor kid must have gone through. What kind of horror and shame he must have felt. Did he call out for help?

And if he did when did the realization come to him that nobody could hear his pleads…I walked…

Walked till my feet began to hurt and rub against the leather of my expensive shoes. Til the soles of my feet and my heels bled. Walked till my sweat drenched my expensive suit.

Walked till that gold watch felt heavy like a shackle upon my wrist and that silk tie began to rub uncomfortably against my neck like that of a noose…and then when I finally reached the steps of my home… When I finally could walk no more… I collapsed. I wept… I didn't weep for that child. Maybe… Maybe I did a little bit but mostly I wept for me. I wept for me…

(The sound of the phone ringing. The MAYOR *appears in a pool of light,* HARRISON *in another.)*

HARRISON: Mrs Mayor.

MAYOR: Turn on the news!

HARRISON: What?

MAYOR: Turn on the news, damnit!!!

HARRISON: What's going on?

MAYOR: You're trying to give me a heart attack is that what this is?
You're trying to give me a fuckin' coronary!
A fuckin' stroke!!!
You're trying to fuckin' kill me!!!

HARRISON: Mrs Mayor?

MAYOR: Don't Mrs Mayor me, you little traitorous fuck. Trying to sabotage my damn election, that's what you're doing. It was you wasn't it?!!

HARRISON: Mrs Mayor, I don't know what you're talking about.

MAYOR: You told the press. You went to the fuckin' press, didn't you?!!!

HARRISON: Oh God.

MAYOR: You leaked it… You let them know. Turn on your tv. Turn on your goddamn TV! I'm going to have your head for this. I swear to god, I'm going to stuff and mount it to a freaking wall.

(Sound of the television turning on)

NEWSCASTER 2: Still no charges have been made as the city stands in the shaky ground between order and chaos.

(Sound of the television channel turning)

NEWSCASTER 1: Thousands are gathering outside of city hall to mourn the tragic rape and death of a young man named Jaxson Price due to what appears to be a lynching by cop.

(Sound of the television changing)

NEWSCASTER 3: We do not know all the details yet. We do not want to speculate but sources inside the police department have reported that the rape and hanging death of a young black male on a playground in Freedman's Town, is believed to have been caused by one of our city's law enforcement officers.

(Sound of the television changing)

NEWSCASTER 2: Tempers and tensions are running high and the call for justice unheard, today the city is starting to look like a police state. We'll keep you posted.

(Sound of the television changing)

NEWSCASTER 3: Growing outrage over a young black male found hanged in a playground as news is revealed that he was raped before his brutal murder took place.

(A PROTESTOR *covering his face with a bandana stands with a Black Lives Matter sign.)*

PROTESTOR: We will accept nothing less than justice. We will not in this lifetime or the next tolerate violence against our citizens, our brothers, our sisters, our neighbors. The news wants to paint us as frustrated. We're not frustrated. We're mad as hell! Mad as hell at the violence being inflicted upon our community by a crooked police department upon people of color.
And if they think we're going to sit down and turn the other god damn cheek they better think again. Cause this ain't our fathers' civil rights movement. We will be heard.

*(*PROTESTOR *sings as the* MAYOR *appears. Over and over she sings as one by one the* NEWSCASTERS *turn into* PROTESTORS *and join in.)*

PROTESTOR:
Mama mama can't you see

What these pigs are doin' to me.
Beatin and abusin' me.
Mama mama can't you see.

(The singing PROTESTOR *removes her bandana covering her face to reveal she's* DAEJAH.*)*

MAYOR: This is a tragedy, a tragedy, plain and simple. This is a tragedy for that young man found hanged on that playground, and this is a tragedy for that police officer being held. We're taking this death personally. If it comes down to it police will be fired, police will be arrested, but none of that will occur until we have answers. We have an election coming up soon, I'm sure that these events have muddied the water for many of you, however let me assure you that it will not stop us from doing everything we can to get ahead of this. That I promise you.

(Lights shift and swirl.)

HARRISON: That night the coroner was forced by the mayor to resign, a group of peaceful protestors marching to join those camped outside of the Mayor's office were tear gassed by the police. A group of four white men in cars waving confederate flags did a drive by in front of the mayor's office and drove off, two people were wounded. Police did nothing. A YouTube clip came out of an officer screaming obscenities and racial slurs at the protestors. The neighborhood bar that served as a police watering hole, which was later revealed to be partially owned by Tomms was burned down in retaliation. Chaos was getting close to breaking out. And I had just a few more days ticking away. Just a few more days before this city would burn.

*(*PROTESTERS *gather by the "Houston Cares" sign and spray paints "Houston Murders",* LIL J's MOMMA *steps out of the*

chaos of voices in a Black Lives Matter T-shirt along with
REVEREND.*)*

REVEREND: Brother and Sisters, thank you all for
coming together today. I'm going to need ya'll to
practice stewardship right with each other. These
police have been slaying Black and Brown, trans, and
abled and disabled across this great nation. It's time we
bring a stop to this. We're coming together to stand by
Jaxson Price's family. We have Jaxson's mother Ja'milla
with us tonight to say a few words. I'm going to ask
that you listen to what she has to say. Come on up here
Ja'milla.

MOMMA: The mayor called me into their pretty office
yesterday. Had me sit down on a comfy little chair next
to his desk overlooking the city. Said she wanted me to
help bring peace to this neighborhood. They said they
want us to come together ya'll! They want a kumbi-yah
moment ya'll! They want me to forgive! A little bit of
amazing grace, and this little light of mine!
They want me to close my eyes. For us to gather hand
in hand and pray the pain away. But I got a different
kind of prayer. Can I tell you my prayer? People can
I tell you my prayer?!! I pray to God above not for
justice. Not for forgiveness. I'm praying for revenge! I
pray to God that the officer that murdered my son. The
officer that beat and violated and hanged my child. I
pray that you toss and turn in your sorrow and never
know sleep. I pray that when that officer opens his
mouth to speak his lies that his tongue turns to razor
blades. And his throat clenches tight and no amount
of water can quench his thirst. I pray that his intestines
turn into snakes and devour you from the inside out
and may his blood turns blacker than the skin of those
he's oppressed.
May your seed decay inside of you and may your
fingers twist on themselves so that you can never pull

a trigger or put hands upon another Black child again.
I pray that when you beg God for forgiveness that he
turns his back on you. That every step you take you
never feel safety in your shadows. May my son and the
death of all those who have been murdered by police
haunt your soul and one day when you find yourself
broken and alone, and you think just for a moment that
you've escaped your past I PRAY that the spirits of:
Eric Garner, Michael Brown, Alton Sterling, Manuel
Loggins,
Sandra Bland, Trayvon Martin, Jamar Clark,
Rekia Boyd, Sean Bell, Walter Scott,
Amadou Diallo, Freddie Gray,
My son
And more, and more, and more
And more, and thousands more long forgotten
Rise up from your shadow and claw away at your flesh
And pull you into the darkness from whence you
came.
Binding your soul forever.
That is my PRAYER!!!
So, I got a question for you mayor. You going to get my
baby, justice? Or is it up to the community to go take
it?!!!

(*A whistle blows and police rush the* PROTESTORS *there's a
fight that ensues. The woman is hit by a police officer, and
blood spills. The police push the protestors back.* HARRISON
appears.)

(*He sees the blood on the ground, takes out a handkerchief
and wipes the blood off the floor and holds it tight.*)

HARRISON: We have to live in this neighborhood. The
people deserve to know to the truth.

(He turns to leave and stops as LIL J *emerges from the shadows. They look at each other before* HARRISON *turns towards the audience.)*

END OF ACT ONE

ACT TWO

Third Movement

(Cold darkness as shadowy of figures moving forward in darkness united carrying signs. They move slowly, voices rising louder and louder. An ocean of voices)

PROTESTOR: Brothas and sistas!!!

CHORUS: Yeah!!

PROTESTOR: Brothas and sistas!!!

CHORUS: Yeah!!!

PROTESTOR: Let them hear you say we want justice!!!

CHORUS: We want justice!!!

PROTESTOR: When do we want it?

CHORUS: Now!!!

PROTESTOR: We want justice!!!

CHORUS: We want justice!!!!

PROTESTOR: When do we want it?!!!

CHORUS: Now!!!!

PROTESTOR: When do we want it?

CHORUS: Now!!!

PROTESTOR: When do we want it?!!!

CHORUS: NOW!!!

*(Lights shift and swirl. The sound of the gavel hits once...
twice...three times.)*

HARRISON: My dad, wise man that he was, always
use to say that Houston is so damn hot, it's where
the devil goes for vacation. I think that's true. There's
just something about August heat that causes men
and women to lose their minds. Three months till the
election. Protestors were now camped out in front of
the Mayor's office. I get a call from my wife yesterday
morning.
That a package was mailed to our house. "Package?" I
said. She said she placed it on our bed for me to open
once I get home. Said it felt like a box of some kind.
Heavy...must be important. She said. I get home, open
my door, race up the stairs and down the hall to our
bedroom. And there it is on our bed. Ordinary box.
Cardboard. Sealed tight with tape. No return address.
Just my name scribbled on the top. Fear in my throat.
Stay calm. Don't frighten her. I think of an excuse. Any
excuse. A mindless errand to get my pregnant wife
out the house. I wait to hear her car pulling out of our
driveway. Thank God. I take a deep breath, sit on the
bed and...I open it and a lifeless rat drops onto our
bed. Another message from our neighborhood police.
I'm getting the hint.

(MAYOR's office. The sound of protestors outside.)

MAYOR: Their growing. Jesus Christ their growing.
Why won't these people just go the hell home?
Madness...absolute madness out there. This must end,
and this must end now.

HARRISON: What are you doing?

MAYOR: I'm calling the damn National Guard. What's
it look like I'm doing?

HARRISON: Put down the phone Mrs Mayor.

MAYOR: They burnt down a bar, Harrison. They've
flipped over a damn cop car. You know what's next?
They'll burn down a Walgreens, a Grocery store,
maybe trek to River Oaks or worse to my house. This
type of thing doesn't happen here. It won't happen
here. Cleveland, Baltimore, L A, but not here... Not
here damnit... We haven't had a race riot in this town
since 1978, and I'll be damned if another one happens
on my watch. I'm not going to have that haunt my
legacy. Rules is what separates us from the animals.

HARRISON: Mrs Mayor, Mrs Mayor, damnit Charli,
put down the phone and listen to me. You know what
pushed those cities over the edge. It was calling in the
National Guard. That's what pushed it into madness.
What does it look like if we start patrolling those
streets with armored trucks and machine guns? You
think about that.

MAYOR: What other choice do I have?

HARRISON: The protestors are peaceful, you can't lump
them all together just because of a few fringe groups
misbehaving...

MAYOR: You actually believe that or are you just saying
that cause poor mourning mother Ms Price is out there
leading the damn protest? Didn't think I knew that did
you?

HARRISON: She has every right to be angry.
Madame Mayor put your faith in me. I can get the reins
of this, I can get control of this if you let me.

(*The* MAYOR *sighs and puts down the phone.*)

MAYOR: What are you proposing?

HARRISON: Tomms has a file of complaints against
him that is damn near two inches thick and you didn't
think its worth mentioning. Heller is our primary
suspect for this crime. The cops aren't going to break

their precious blue wall. We need to do this the right way. I can't play this handcuffed any longer. I need you to let me loose. I can't play the politic game and get justice for this kid at the same time. The higher ups, the police unions, the officers themselves. You put me on this case for a reason. Let me loose.

MAYOR: Let you loose? Like some sort of unchained dog?

HARRISON: We have two months left. Just two months till election. Just let me do my job.

MAYOR: I used to have this dog. I didn't...rather it was my wife's. Little yippy thing, she named it Putt-Putt. Can you imagine the hell of walking that dog to the park and yelling its name? Come here Putt-Putt. Putt-Putt sit. Putt-Putt behave. Hard to respect a woman who walks a dog named Putt-Putt. Hell, it's hard to respect a dog named Putt-Putt.

HARRISON: I don't see what this has to do with anything.

MAYOR: So, my wife. Love her to death but she's not a dog person. You can tell when someone's not a dog person. Mutt needs to be walked at six, she gets up at nine. Doesn't rub the dog nose in the piss spot when it marks its territory in the damn house. Doesn't come when you call him. Barks at every damn thing imaginable. You tell lil Putt-Putt to sit, the bastard will roll over. You tell him to stop barking, he'll bark louder, tell him to stay, he'll go. It's because he wasn't house broken. Got so bad we had to put diapers on the damn dog. One day I'm walking the little disobedient bastard and we happen upon our neighbor, a good friend of mine, comes by fixes my satellite when I can't get it to act right, always has his wife bring me this wonderful pecan pie that if you taste it is
(Kisses the sky)

to die for, give you the shirt off his back. Anyway, we come up on my neighbor me and this dog and I said stay… That little fuck dog bites the man. Breaks the skin.

You know what happens then…I call say hey the dish seems to be acting up, he's suddenly busy, the sky pours down rain, I spill some barbeque sauce on my shirt no more borrowing of his, and most importantly no more of that delicious pecan pie. I tell my wife take that mutt dog to get trained she'd never did it. Finally, I just had enough. I took that little Putt-Putt for a walk along the bayou, after we walked awhile I unchained that dog from its leash, stroked that dog's piss stained furry little body, picked it up, looked into its eyes lovingly and then punted little Putt-Putt as hard as I could into the water to be a snack for the gators…Told my wife a bald eagle swooped down from the sky and grabbed it. Police union is donating two million to my campaign, the Police Fraternity is donating one-point-five million, these protestors…

Hell, I don't even think half of them have paid taxes in the last five years. Do you understand the math here? Don't get in the way of my pecan pie. By the way how's things with the wife?

HARRISON: I don't see how that has anything to do with anything.

MAYOR: Just answer the question.

HARRISON: We're fine…

MAYOR: Don't lie to me… A little bird told me that you slept in the office last night. Want to become Mayor one day? Make sure that your domestic headaches don't spill over into work.

HARRISON: This case is… It might be causing some… strain.

MAYOR: I can imagine. You know when I first met you. You were this brat of a kid, an absolute know it all, but I saw in those eyes this intense fire in you, like you dreamed of this world differently than everyone else...I said that boy, he's going to be mayor one day. And if I didn't want to be on the losing side I better train you up. Create you into my image. And you know over the last few years I can't say just how truly proud I am of you. I feel like so much of your success is because I've believed in what you are capable of. I like to think I've done a damn good job so far...I see it in you, you know that... The ability to one day sit in the big chair, but you haven't realized one thing yet. There's something important that you haven't quite figured out... Being mayor isn't about the speeches, the media, the countless photo ops, kissing filthy babies, and pressing flesh with bastards you don't give a damn about. It's about playing the game. Moving one piece one way, and another an opposite way to ensure that every time you step to the board you check mate your opposition. You haven't figured that out yet. You get me answers, you bring this to a close before election day, but you play within the parameters I've given you. You understand me. Too many pieces are at play, and I can't have you messing up the game for me. Especially this close to the election. You play the game how I tell you. With the moves your pawn is allowed to go. In other words, do your job but don't disturb the order of things.

HARRISON: I'm more than capable of doing my job.

MAYOR: Of course, you can, Putt-Putt, that's what I'm banking on.
You can go now. Remember to stay on your leash. You only get one chance to bite me.

(HELLER *picks up phone.*)

Zeida, sweetie, thank God you haven't left for lunch yet...look sweetheart do me a favor, can you have one of the interns run down to the bakery get me a dozen sprinkle donuts. But hey do me a favor. I need you to do this cause those interns...those interns never get it right. I want you to pick out the red sprinkles. Yeah no...Zeida. You're the only one I trust to be able to do this. Thank you, you're a life saver.

Lights shift. Harrison finds himself standing alone.

HARRISON: I dreamt that night. Same dream as always. The boy standing in darkness, the arms outstretched, the thousands gathered...the drowning in blood. But this time...I somehow wash ashore gasping and choking for breath. And I find myself upon this shore filled with thousands of sun bleached bones littered the sandy shore. And I look and in the distance there I see Lil J standing in the doorway. And he had this look of quiet desperation in his eyes, and he mouths the words "Speak for me."

(Lights shift.)

(REVEREND appears.)

REVEREND: Mr Just.

HARRISON: Yes, Reverend.

REVEREND: I...I think I know where you can find someone who can help you.

HARRISON: You do? That would be amazing. Who is it?

(Lights shift and swirl.)

(Interrogation room)

HELLER: What are you doing here?

HARRISON: Just thought I should let you know that I have a witness.

HELLER: You do?

HARRISON: They're willing to come forward.

HELLER: That's interesting developments.

HARRISON: I like to think so. You know I'm feeling generous. This could be a chance for you. A chance to make thing right. I'm willing to be lenient. Confess to the crime of killing Jaxson Price. Or let me know it was Tomms. You don't have to have your life destroyed by this.

HELLER: My life is already destroyed.

HARRISON: All I want is justice. I don't know what happened that night. The details behind the incident are so horrible I...I struggle to look at you. You can do what's right. You can bring this story to a close.

HELLER: I don't care about whatever *your* witness has to say.
I don't give a damn about what some street rat might have seen.
You think it's going to matter if some punk boy tells you anything.
You think it's going to make a difference?
I know my truth.
This interview is over.
(*He turns to leave.*)

HARRISON: Heller.
I never said the witness was a boy.

(*Silence*)

HELLER: You know I've been thinking a lot about that Jaxson boy lately.
I did what I thought was right. And I get thrown into a cell. The same cell that I threw that boy into time after time after time.

(*The sound of jail doors sliding shut.*)

(*LIL J is thrown into the cell with another man.*)

LIL J: Hey, I want my phone! Hey sir, can I get my phone call?

I just want to go home.

God please help me.

God please just help me out.

The Lord is my shepherd I shall not want—

CAPITÁN: Hey boi king you aight? Wah gwan lil' lion? Talk to me... You alright?

LIL J: Yeah, I'm cool... It stinks in here.

CAPITÁN: Yeah, they do it to make you think you an animal to make you feel like less than human. Leave us in here with piss, shit, and flies. Stench of oppression. Force feed us memories of slave ships...that's what they do... Push us from one cell to the next. Like we cattle. Like we three-fifths a man. They do this on purpose. Fuckin' Babylonian pigs. You scurred huh? It's okay you can be scurred. First time they threw me in here I was scared to death. Know what I mean. You don't mind me askin' what you in here for?

LIL J: Hanging out in the park after hours.

CAPITÁN: You shittin' me?

LIL J: No.

CAPITÁN: Fuckin' America. Can't even get fresh air without being harassed. Fresh air is free. They throw you in jail for being in a damn park?

LIL J: Yeah.

CAPITÁN: No guns, no knives, no W M Ds? Just getting fresh air? As a tax paying American citizen... In a public park?

LIL J: Yeah.

CAPITÁN: Muthaphuckas!!! They going to waste our tax paying dollars for some bullshit like that. Come on. You weren't doing anything wrong and they arrest you for that. They make a profit out of us, boi king. That the truth… Locking us up and then making us pay to get out. You know what they arrest me for? You want to know? Over a spork!

LIL J: Spork?

CAPITÁN: Yeah, yeah, you know a spork? Part spoon, part fork. Spork. Anyway, yeah, boi king, me go to one of them white people chicken places. That should have been first sign of trouble, cause what them white people know about chicken in first place? Me ask for a three piece and a biscuit.
Hand them people me money, and then what they do? What they do? They give me little lil' chickens and guess what…no biscuits. Me couldn't be mad about the chicken, me thinks maybe that's just how white people like they chicken, but the biscuit… No no no no so me go up to man, and me say hey sir, you ain't give me no biscuit. He say you must have ate it. Me ask the man is he callin' me a liar and he just smirks at me. Me said excuse me sir, is you calling me a liar… He smirks at me like he sittin' in the big chair, looking down at me in a low low place. And he smirks and say, "I guess so." What me do? Me stabbed that sommabitch with a spork.

LIL J: With a spork?

CAPITÁN: Damn right. Anyway, so he screamin', callin' out to dear Jesus. Me say what you screamin' for? Damn thing didn't break no skin, you not bleedin' none… Serves you right callin' me liar.
Next thing me know three cops roll up on me pushing me around. Saying me assaultin' the fool man. Me say me not assaultin' shit. Me know my fuckin' right. He called to me face, me a liar. He assaulted me. Now look at me. Stuck in this nasty muthaphucka!
(To the unseen)

You sons of bitches could clean this damn thing out
some time!!!
Got us in here like animals!!! Like freakin' caged
animals!!!
Me a human, he's a human... we're human beings and
you got us in this filth! In this filth like this.
(To LIL J*)*
And you know what man, what so crazy about the
damn thing.
Me was on my way to fuckin job interview. Job
interview, so me could be an upright American
citizen... Get this... At a damn chicken place. And you
bastards ruined that for me!!! Wasn't gonna get the
damn thing anyway but me was on my way. Shiiit.
God bless fuckin' America. Say boi king what's your
name?

LIL J: They call me Lil J

CAPITÁN: Lil J, Lil J, Lil J... Me going to call you boi
king.
Cause that's what you are. Boi king. Yeah lil' lion, you
a boi king, I'm start callin' you...
My name is Sinbad James. My friends call me Capitán.
So, ya can call me Capitán, eh!
You get your phone call?

LIL J: No?

CAPITÁN: Man, they fuckin' up. They supposed to give
you a phone call. That's your right as an American you
know. They not supposed to throw you in this hell hole
and not give you a phone call.
Hey boi king? You stay strong. Alright. Me gotcha.
Stick close to me.
(To the unseen)
Hey! You suppose to give the boi king a phone call.
Hey! Hey! Hey don't ignore me! You see me talkin'

to you, you steroid no neck muthaphuckas. You can't throw us in here and treat us this way. Like animals. We are God's creatures. You can't fuckin' do that! You can't abuse God's creatures!!! What you think we don't know what our rights are?!! Me see you Babylonian pig and I see your evil ways! You say in God we trust but you lie!!! Babylonian pigs you lie. Filthy as this jail cell you hold me in, your souls are! Babylonian pigs!!! God is a God of love!!! And he has turned his back on your cruelty. You want me to stand and kiss this country but I spit on you!!! I spit on your cruelty!!! I spit on this city and how you treat your people! I spit on your government! I spit on your America!!! I spit on your America!!! The Atlantic was a pond, A pond... before me ancestors filled it with their tears, the tears you brought they way... Me pray that the Pacific and the Atlantic decide to kiss. And drown your evil ways in the same tears me ancestors done cried...

Drown your Houston, drown your Cleveland, drown your New York, Drown your Chicago, your Baltimore, the whole evil state of Florida... Drown it in the tears of my ancestors and wash it clean off the map. And you know what all the Blacks, the Asians, the Indians, the Middle Easterns, the fuckin' Natives, oh we gonna float!!! We gonna float to the top, basking in the sun light, while you fuckin' drown! And we gonna thank you for teachin' us how to swim, you Babylonian pigs!!! Cause you taught us how to swim in the evil you try pouring down our throats!!! No no no... There will be a revolution that comes, you can believe that!!! And when it comes I will dance. I will dance on your false American flag and raise up a new one!!! I will raise up a flag of love! I will raise up a flag of peace! I will raise up a flag for a new America!!! A True AMERICA WHERE ALL MEN ARE CREATED EQUAL!!! I WILL RAISE IT UP!!!

(Lights shift and swirl.)

(HELLER *and* TOMMS.*)*

TOMMS: What you call me in here for?

HELLER: I can't keep doing this.

TOMMS: What are you talking about?

HELLER: Please don't be mad at me... Please...don't be
mad... But I can't do this...I can't keep doing this...
I just see that kid. Every time I close my eyes...I just
see... Him...

TOMMS: Who?

HELLER: The boy... Him on that swing. Tangled. I
just—

TOMMS: Sssssshhh... Sssshhh... Sssshhh...
Hold out just a little bit longer kid. The badge is on our
side. Never forget that. It's on our side.

HELLER: I want to tell them.

TOMMS: You keep your mouth shut.

HELLER: I can't keep carrying this weight on me. I'm
not sleeping.

TOMMS: Then buy you some fuckin' Nyquil... You hear
me. You keep your mouth shut. Mouth. Fuckin'. Shut.

HELLER: Look at me I'm all over the place. They're
saying they got a witness.

TOMMS: Pull yourself together. They don't have shit.
That's a scare tactic. They're trying to bait you. They
see you tie that swing set around that kids' neck? They
see you strangle that kid till the life left his body? No.
No they didn't. All they have...that is if they have
anything is you out at the park near the body. Means
nothing. Cops are near dead bodies all the damn time,
rookie. They don't have nothing. We didn't kill that
kid. Repeat after me we didn't kill that kid.

HELLER: But... But...I got to tell them...I got to tell them... This guy he knows. They already know. We did that to him.

TOMMS: Got a wife? Got a kid?

HELLER: You know I don't.

TOMMS: WELL I FUCKING DO!!!
You stay the goddamn course. You don't fuckin' stray. You don't fuckin' deviate. Haven't the union been looking out for you? Haven't I been looking out for you? When you were just a pup on this damn job wasn't it me that took you under my wing? When they finally let you out and you were bitching and moaning about how you'd never be able to pay those bills who talked to the captain to put you on the desk?

HELLER: You did.

TOMMS: Yeah me... Cushy gig right, you just got to kick back shuffle a few papers, drink a few beers and poke a few of the badge bunnies, right? You've had a week and half of vacation, so far kid. I've been looking out for you... Always been looking out for you, haven't I?

HELLER: Yeah.

TOMMS: Yeah, I have...and always will... So, believe me when I tell you keep your fuckin' mouth shut. They don't have a case. You hear me... They don't have nothing on us.

(Lights swirl.)

Fourth Movement

(Lights swirl and shift. The sound of protestors grows.)

(MOMMA enters as HARRISON goes over some documents.)

HARRISON: Thank you for seeing me on such short notice.

MOMMA: I ain't had much choice with them cops bangin' at my door like that. Now did I?

HARRISON: I apologize about that. I honestly do. I hope they showed you the respect that you deserve.

MOMMA: What's done is done and now here we find ourselves. You over there rocking your nice suit, all college educated, and speaking the queen's fuckin' English.
What you call me here for? Let me guess you wanted to let me know you plannin' on standing by the ones who are helping with the funneling of the school house to the jail house industry. Is that what you wanted to tell me?

HARRISON: You think I'm not conflicted by this situation?

MOMMA: I think the same government that paid the police that murdered my son are the exact same ones that pay your check too. I watch the news, Mr Just, I look at social media. Time after time, what do I see? Cop kills young black kid from poor neighborhood like Freedman's Town. Kills some kid just like my son, Jaxson Price. People like you don't care about a people like my son. His life doesn't matter when the city is considering how much money they can make from increasing property taxes, gerrymandering voting districts, urban renewal, gentrification, and every other big S A T word they can profit with. I was a fool to believe otherwise.

HARRISON: Ms Price, you are right. When I first took this case, I did feel that way. Just like you, I've seen those countless young black boys and girls snatched away from this world far beyond their time. I asked myself, "Why take this case on? Their cops...nothing ever happens to cops." But the more I watched as you pour out your soul to the people for the son that you lost. For a life that didn't need to be snatched away, it made me think about my mother, and my grandma still living in Freedman's Town, it made me think about my wife.

It made me think about the woman that I love and the child that she's carrying inside of her. Our child and it made me think of what she would go through if something happened to our child. It made me see that I need to speak out and fight back in whatever way that I can. And for me the best way I know how to fight is by stepping into that court room. You've given up on the system, that's fair, but don't give up on me. I'm standing right here and I'm going to get you justice.

MOMMA: It was you wasn't it? You leaked the news about what they had done to my baby didn't you?

HARRISON: …

MOMMA: What do you need from me?

HARRISON: Tell me about Daijah?

MOMMA: How you know about her?

HARRISON: She was J's girl? The girl he'd use to meet at night in the playground?

MOMMA: I don't wanna talk about her.

HARRISON: Ma'am…
Ma'am, look at me.
You say you want to get justice for your son.
Well so do I. By you telling me about this girl, can open this case up for me.

MOMMA: I tell you about that girl, then that opens door. And I'm not about to shit on my son's grave like that.

HARRISON: Well there are things that need to be answered and if you can provide the picture of who J truly was then we can get a full picture of what happened. There's a chance for you to help me be the one who put those people who killed your son away. Tell me about Jaxson and Daijah.
Can you do that? Talk to me.

MOMMA: Well first to understand J, you got to realize his life was one big tragicomedy
Everyone in his world except me was droppin' like flies on him. His daddy was a good man died from a broken-soul disease, crazy young age, and then you remember that shooting that went down a couple years back of Big E?

HARRISON: Big E?

MOMMA: Yeah Big E, ummm Eric Strong. Cops killed him shot him twenty times because he was reaching for his wallet? Yeah so that was like his hero. So, everyone he ever cared about was droppin' on him. And then he met Daejah., and man, Daejah was like...

(LIL J *appears from the darkness. The sound of wind chimes and* DAEJAH *follows behind him soon after.*)

LIL J: Hey

DAEJAH: Hey yourself.

MOMMA: Peace in the storm. That quiet that you pray to come when that cruel darkness beats against you. She was good for that boy.

DAEJAH: I was wondering when you'd get here.

LIL J: Had to make sure the cops weren't circling around the playground first.

DAEJAH: Smart cookie.

LIL J: Speaking of cookies.

DAEJAH: You trying to get you a nibble.

LIL J: I'm hungry for more than just a nibble.

DAEJAH: You nasty.

LIL J: Yeah but you like it.

MOMMA: I'm telling you those two were perfect for each other. Daejah's delicate like a flower on the outside but man she was rock solid you know. I could tell she was destined to grow into the definition of a strong black woman and that's what J needed in his life.

LIL J: I saved up some more funds

DAEJAH: You did?

LIL J: Hell yeah! We can leave this place tomorrow if we wanted to. Never look back.

DAEJAH: But our families.

LIL J: Hell, with them. It'll be us. Free! I can see it.

MOMMA: Daejah was strong.

DAEJAH: Don't say that. Who are we without family? Have you worked things out with your momma?

LIL J: No.

DAEJAH: Well I'm not going anywhere till you do.

LIL J: Dae—

DAEJAH: I'm putting my foot down. We. Aren't. Leaving. Till. You. Make. Peace.

LIL J: Why you being like that? Only thing I need in this life is standing right in front of me.

DAEJAH: Cause I don't want you to leave here with that hanging over you.
Anyhow…I love you

LIL J: You aight.

MOMMA: One day Daejah is hanging out with him and their friends, at the playground cause that's what them children tend to do. At night. You know? To get away from the parents. The world. The craziness. That was their thing. And this car drives up. Dark windows.

LIL J: Smart ass

DAEJAH: It's a beautiful ass.

LIL J: Yeah it is.

MOMMA: Tires squealing.

DAEJAH: I got to get going soon.

LIL J: Do you have to?

DAEJAH: Suns almost up.
You be careful with that money, J.

LIL J: I'm not going to let anybody take our future away. Put some faith in me I'm an entre-po-negro.

DAEJAH: That a promise?

LIL J: You know it.

MOMMA: This door swings open and this man comes running towards for God knows what reason and he slams J against the wall. And they're like "What the hell is going on?" And he's yelling at them, searching J's pockets. Pushing them and roughing them children up. And Daejah she's not having it. She's not having it at all.

LIL J: Can I see you tomorrow?

DAEJAH: I don't know… You going to make peace with your momma?

MOMMA: And she calls this guy out. Cussing him out. And it turns out this guy is some off-duty cop. What he was doing? I don't know playing batman or something who the hell knows?

LIL J: For you yes.

DAEJAH: Then yeah, I'll see you tomorrow then.

MOMMA: So Daejah is like "I know my right. I want your name and I want your badge number." And the children with were telling her to shut up. Cause they've grown to know how these racist cops act if you call them out on their shit. But she's still going. Strong young woman child.

LIL J: Hey before you go.

DAEJAH: Yeah

LIL J: Come here.

MOMMA: And I don't know if he was just trying to scare her or he really meant to do it. But he pulls out his gun. That cop pulls out his gun and…

DAEJAH: I love you.

MOMMA: Lil J he just held her. Held her tight. Blood everywhere. He's howling, screaming at the moon like some animal, tears streaming down face. Cops and the ambulance people had to pry his fingers off her, he was holding her so tight. And when he couldn't hold her no longer. When he was alone. Alone in the park. Just staring at the darkness. They broke him that night. They broke my son's soul. Just shattered right there that night. He ain't been the same after that. That's what he'd do. Hustle and sell those D V Ds in the morning and then goes out there every other night, sit there for hours, and talk to Daejah. Clutching tight to this gold necklace she once gave him with a butterfly on it and talking to the shadow of her. Her memory I don't know. I don't even know if he knew she was dead. But he'd be there like clockwork. Talking to the darkness until the sun comes up.

(DAEJAH *fades into the darkness.*)

(*Silence. Long silence*)

HARRISON: They killed a girl?

MOMMA: Yeah, they killed a girl. Some cop named Tomms and he walked away scot free too. It doesn't matter to them whether its male or female. They just kill them no thought to it.

(Silence)

HARRISON: A while back you seem certain that Officer Heller was the one that killed Jaxson. My coroner is ruling it as a suicide.

MOMMA: It wasn't no damn suicide.

HARRISON: How can you be so sure?

MOMMA: Cause...

Cause nobody raises hundreds of dollars to leave this town and never look back, only to kill themselves.

HARRISON: What do you mean?

MOMMA: That boy sold those D V Ds and he kept that money hidden.

HARRISON: Why didn't you tell anyone?

MOMMA: Just did. Bet you check them officers bank accounts one of them going have a bunch of new money in there that can't be accounted for.

HARRISON: I'm sorry that not going to do it. With that small amount of money they can easily say they got that from anywhere. I thought you'd be able to provide me with something else to help crack this.

MOMMA: Well, there's my baby's necklace that he prized more than anything in the world. It was missing when I had to claim his body. He never took it off ever. You know I had to bury him without that necklace. He wouldn't have wanted to go anywhere without.

HARRISON: Can you remember what this necklace look like?

(Lights fade away on MOMMA.*)*

(HARRISON *and* HELLER.*)*

HARRISON: Time to be a man and come clean.

HELLER: I don't know what you're talking about?

HARRISON: Finally found out the victim was raped with a police baton before his death. We search yours or Tomms' baton who's going to come up clean?

HELLER: Fuck you. I do good police work.

HARRISON: You're going to fit in real nicely with the prison population.

HELLER: This isn't right.

HARRISON: What you think we weren't going to discover that?
You murdered that kid. For what a few hundred dollars he kept in a rusty can?
What happened? Started off just trying to teach the guy a lesson and just went too far?
Or maybe you intended to kill him all along.

HELLER: You don't fuckin' talk to me like that!

HARRISON: Or what? You gonna try and rape me with a police baton?

HELLER: You don't know me.

HARRISON: Admit what you did.
Be a man! Look me in the eye. And tell me that all the things in this report is not true.
You beat him half to death.
You beat him bloody, like an animal… Like he was nothing more than some animal to abuse and then…
Stole his money like some kind of common crook before you sodomized the poor kid, wrapped him in chains and hanged him.
You lynched a young boy for what?

To make some kind of statement to the community?
Cause he made you fill out too much paper work?!!
Look me in the eye like a man and tell why you did it.

HELLER: We're done here.

HARRISON: Yeah, we're done. You're a disgrace to the
badge. A disgrace to the uniform.

HELLER: I want a rep.
I want to hire a lawyer.

HARRISON: Oh, now you want to lawyer?!!

HELLER: I didn't kill that kid.
(He pulls at his shirt collar.)

HARRISON: Mind telling me why you keep pulling at
your collar all the time? Got a noose around your neck?

HELLER: Go to hell.

HARRISON: Was it Tomms?!! Was it you?!! Who was it?

*(HARRISON grabs HELLER, HELLER pushes back, and
HARRISON yanks a necklace off. It's LIL J's.)*

HELLER: Are you crazy? Get off me. Get off me!

(HARRISON picks up the necklace.)

HARRISON: Where'd you get this?
Heller, where'd you get this from? A gold necklace
with a butterfly pendant.

HELLER: Give that back.

HARRISON: That's Jaxson Price's necklace.

HELLER: That's mine.

HARRISON: You took this off that boy didn't you?
Didn't you?!!
What are you doing with this?

(HELLER breaks down into tears.)

HELLER: It's a war zone, I like to take souvenirs from the battlefield.

HARRISON: I think you have some explaining you need to do.

HELLER: We were just tired of always...the fuckin' kid. All those reports, always dragging him home. Tossing him in the cell didn't work...Tomms had enough.

HARRISON: So Tomms was involved.

(Lights shift and swirl.)

HELLER: He was out there again, and we told him to get going. The kid—

HARRISON: Jaxson.

HELLER: Yeah, he...well... We were trying to get Jaxson to go home since it was about to be some rough weather coming. And Jaxson...fuckin' kid he has to go and get smart with Tomms. For what reason I don't fuckin' know.

(LIL J appears.)

TOMMS: When you gonna learn you little shit? Go home.

LIL J: When you gonna lose some fuckin' weight, you donut eating fat shit?

TOMMS: What you say to me?

LIL J: I said you can get back in your car and leave me alone.

TOMMS: Who do you think you talkin' to?

HELLER: Jaxson. Just do what the man says and get going?

LIL J: I'm waiting for my girl. I haven't had the chance to talk to her yet. She'll be mad if I'm not here when she shows.

TOMMS: This kid is a fuckin' crazy farm. I've had about enough of his shit.

HELLER: God damn it.

TOMMS: I'm so close to writing your ass a ticket right now.

LIL J: Then write me a ticket and let me go about my way.
You say you want me to go home. Well I will. Just let me say see my girl first.
And then I'll go home to my momma.

TOMMS: I'm not going to repeat myself again to you. You get going.

LIL J: This is harassment.
Your harassing me.
Your harassing me for no damn reason.

HELLER: I just snapped you know. I honestly don't know what happened to me. I mean we didn't need this. We had foot chase of a perp earlier that had fired on us. The day before that Tomms had a complaint filed against him by this drug addict. We had responded to a domestic and three separate homicides. Somebody had popped off some rounds at us earlier. We were being told there was the possibility of the city reducing its police force. We were on edge, Freedman's Town was a warzone. And me I was just full out losing my patience with this damn kid. And then he just...
Stupid kid just made me lose it. None of this would have happened if he just...
(To LIL J*)*
Shut up... just shut up.

LIL J: Don't tell me to shut up. I know my rights.
I'm tired of you two over here messing with me.

TOMMS: Hold him.

HELLER: Tomms come on. We don't have to do this today.

TOMMS: No. Hold the little fucker.

LIL J: What you gonna do?
I don't have to do anything. I'm not under arrest.

TOMMS: You are under arrest.

LIL J: For what now?

HELLER: Kid, shut up

LIL J: Sacrificial goat, huh?
Are you fuckin' kidding me? I have the right to know what you are arresting me for.

HELLER: Same thing we've always arrested you for.

TOMMS: That's it. I've had enough of you. I've had enough.
Heller you can't play nice with these fuckin' animals.

LIL J: And you just going to stand there and let him charge me up huh?

HELLER: Look kid we've told you not to come back here or we'll have to lock you up.

TOMMS: You trying to make me angry, is that what you're trying to do?

LIL J: I thought angry was your natural state. Mr Stick up his ass.

HELLER: Do you want us to hurt you or something? Shut the fuck up kid.

LIL J: Both of you are on some bullshit.
Straight up bullshit.
You can't talk to me this way. I'm a boy king. I'm a lion.

(LIL J *spits on* HELLER's *badge.*)

HELLER: Fuckin' hell kid.

(HELLER *pulls out his nightstick and hits* LIL J.)

LIL J: Must feel real manly beating on a black boy huh?

HELLER: I said shut the fuck up.

(HELLER *hits* LIL J *again.*)

TOMMS: Look I want to beat the living hell out of the kid as bad as the next one, but I think that's enough.

(HELLER *hits* LIL J *again.*)

TOMMS: I said that's enough, Heller.

HELLER: Why can't you listen? Why can't you just do what you're told?
(He swings.)
I've been doing nothing but trying to help you and this how you pay me back.
You spit on me. Punk muthaphucka.
(He swings.)
You stupid shit.

TOMMS: Oh, fuck this!
Heller stop, I'm not taking part in this. Leave his ass.

HELLER: He's got to learn man.

(TOMMS *takes a sip from his flask and exits.*)

(HELLER *tires from swinging. Looks down at* LIL J *as he laughs, and blood washed over him.*)

(HELLER *sees the crumpled wad of cash in* LIL J's *balled up fist.*)

HELLER: What's this? Holy shit… Holy shit…
Look at this. There must be what? Seven hundred… eight hundred bucks in here.

LIL J: It's mine. Give it back. It's mine.

HELLER: Possession's nine-tenth of the law you little shit. I'll consider it an early Christmas present.

(LIL J *tries to grab at* HELLER's *pants legs, but he's kicked away.*)

HELLER: Why couldn't you just shut your fuckin' mouth?
(He turns to leave.)

LIL J: Oink oink you piggy.
You don't even know you a bitch.
You don't even know it.

HELLER: What else you got?
(He snatches the butterfly necklace from LIL J.)
Who's walking around wearing a butterfly on their necklace, huh?

LIL J: Give it back.

HELLER: Nah, think I'm going to keep this. Time you learn a lesson.
You stupid fuck. You stupid fuckin' animal... I'll show you who's a bitch.

(HELLER *climbs a top* LIL J. *Places his knee on his back and raising the baton high)*
(Darkness. Cold hard. Cruel darkness)
(It feels like an eternity.)
(The sound of a low ringing sounds)
(DAEJAH *appears.*)

DAEJAH: J?!! J baby!

LIL J: They took it.

DAEJAH: They took what?

LIL J: They took our money. They took your necklace.

DAEJAH: Sssssshhh...

LIL J: They took it.

DAEJAH: Hey…hey…sssshhh…ssssshhh… Let's go
home. We can go home. We can go home.

LIL J: They took everything from me. What's there to
go home to? What's there to go home to? Nothing. I
have nothing. Let's leave this place, Daejah. Let's leave
here and never come back.

DAEJAH: Ssssshh we can't.

LIL J: Why not? I don't want to be in this place no more.
I don't want to be here. I want to be with you. That's all
I want. All the hatred. All the cruelty. All the evil this
city carries like cancer. I just want to be free of it. Away
from this place. Away from all this concrete where
nothing grows but weeds. I'm going to get us out of
here. We going to get outta here. I promise you that.
We going to get out of here.

DAEJAH: It can't be that way.

LIL J: Why not?

DAEJAH: You know why?

LIL J: I don't.

DAEJAH: No. You know. Say it.

LIL J: I can't

DAEJAH: Say it.

LIL J: Why do I have to say it? Why do I have to say it?

DAEJAH: Cause you need to know that you can't bring
me back. Say it.

LIL J: I can't. I can't say…

DAEJAH: Why can't you say it?

LIL J: Because if I say it, then I'm alone in this world.
Then there's nothing for me to hold on to…

DAEJAH: Say the words.

LIL J: I'm not going to say it.

DAEJAH: You're tired.

LIL J: I'm tired.

DAEJAH: You should come home to me, Jaxson.

LIL J: But how?

DAEJAH: Just say the thing you've struggled for so long to say.

LIL J: My soul shattered when you left. I miss the smell of you. And your laugh. I miss you...

DAEJAH: And?

LIL J: Your dead and I never told you... I never told you that I love you. I've always loved you.

DAEJAH: There was that so hard? Let's go home. Let's go home Jaxson.

(LIL J *walks to his secret place and pulls out a backpack. Tears stream down his face. Pain filled sobs. He pulls from his backpack, a liquor bottle and drinks. Drinks hard. Chokes on it... He drinks from it again slower this time.*)

(*He wipes his mouth and his eyes. Looks up towards the sky...and begins to cry once again. Thunder and lightning. He screams before he rises to his feet and calms himself. He turns to leave and then stops himself. He walks up to the swing set and bangs his head against the railing once, twice, three times. Fighting back tears before breaking out into heavy harsh sobs. He takes the swings and wraps it first around his hands, then around his neck, pulls it tightly around him and pulls himself down upon it. He gasps for breath and rage screams, he stops...*)

(*He pulls against the weight of the swing set and again screams as his body fights for breath.... One by one images of those who have been killed by police brutality flash upon the stage intersected with images of lynchings throughout American history constantly flashing back and forth across the screen. Faster the heart beats pulsing, racing and finally*)

as the sound and the images becomes unbearable to watch.
He pulls against his chains...roars as the last of his life
leaves his body, the last of his energy he pulls his feet up and
let his life be yanked from him. Chains and body tangled
alone on the playground.)

(Silence)

(Silence)

(Silence)

(Painful silence)

(Lights shift and swirl)

NEWSCASTER 2: The grand jury concluded with a
unanimous decision of guilty on both Tomms and
Heller. They'll be sentences to six months in jail.

(Lights shift and swirl. HARRISON appears. He unties his
tie, he tucks his shirt. Strips off his suit coat)

HARRISON: Six months in jail. I fought for more. I
honestly did.
But my employers...the city said...

MAYOR: We can't make it seem as if every little thing
that the police do in the line of duty will get them
thrown into jail. If that happens they'll never do any
policing. What type of message does that send our
boys in blue. We need both the community and the
police to be better citizens to each other. That's the
only way this can be changed. It's tragic about what
happened to that young man... but at the end of the
day we're giving this community, the justice they've
been calling for.

HARRISON: Justice. Is that what that looks like?

(Lights shift to HARRISON and the MAYOR in the office.)

MAYOR: Thank you for seeing me. Sorry to hear that
you are stepping down. You've been an asset to this
administration.

HARRISON: Why do I get the feeling that there is a "but" to follow that statement?

MAYOR: Well, of course you know by you resigning means that I can't endorse you if you should at the end of my next term decide to run for the office. I mean it's not good for the optics.

HARRISON: Optics? Optics. You're concerned about optics. Why aren't you concerned about keeping your word. Unbelievable. Charli, absolutely unbelievable. I did what you wanted. I wrapped the case before the election. I put myself and my family on the line to get justice. And...and this is how you play things? I did my damn job!

MAYOR: Is that what you call it?

HARRISON: Yeah, that's exactly what I'd call it. We made an agreement Charli.

MAYOR: And I am the mayor, and any and all promises and agreements I can honor or not at my discretion

HARRISON: Who are you Charli?!!

MAYOR: Listen to me the first time. I'm the mayor! I told you to stay on your leash! You think I wasn't going to find out about that leak? About you supporting McHenry and that grieving mother. Think I didn't see you trying to play hero?

HARRISON: I was doing what was right for my community.

MAYOR: I don't care about what is right and wrong for the community! I have to keep this city moving forward towards progress.

HARRISON: At who's cost? Who gets plowed over for the sake of the city? For progress Charli?

MAYOR: I want you to pay very close attention to me when I say this to you.

You sat in the District Attorney's office at my whim.
My say was what put you in that office. To serve not
some crying mother, not the community of Freedman's
Town, not the city of Houston, but me.
I said I wanted this wrapped with a neat and tidy bow.
Nothing about this was neat. You made this job vastly
more difficult, Harrison.
Then you stepped down when the chips didn't fall
how you liked it.
And because of that failing you won't see any
endorsement to become my predecessor coming from
this office. In fact, if I was you don't even think about
running, you wanted to be the great black savior, well,
have at it but in the process you've made yourself a
pariah. You can see yourself out my office now.

(HARRISON begins to leave.)

MAYOR: Oh, and by the way. I want you keep this in
mind. You ever cross me again, stand in the way of
progress again and you'll discover there's far scarier
things that I can have dropped at your door than a
dead rat in box.

(Lights shift to HARRISON standing alone.)

*(He moves to the playground and stands besides the swing
set that LIL J once hanged from.)*

HARRISON: Did I make a mistake? Was standing up and
seeking out justice for Lil J's mother the wrong move
to make? I don't believe that it was. I refuse to believe
that.

*(As HARRISON speaks one by one he's joined by the
multitude voices gathering together in the distance lighting
candles and carrying protest signs.)*

(REVEREND and MOMMA locked arm in arm behind him.)

HARRISON: A life was taken.

And his voice, his story, and all the others taken away
before their time need…
I did what was right.
I stood up.
I saw the truth and…
I fought.
I admit I was reluctant at first to take this case, the
mayor was right,
normally you do become some kind of a political
pariah
Speaking out for the unheard, often you become
viewed as the troublemaker.
But I'm not playing politics game their way no more.
Not how they play it.
Will I win the mayor's office?
I don't know.
What I can say with confidence as I'm speaking to you
right now.
Is that the polls have me one point behind our current
mayor.
Guess she shouldn't have let me off her leash.
But regardless whether I win this campaign or not.
I'll fight for this community.
I'll stand up. I'll speak out.
Till all the dying voices are heard.

(The group of gathering in the shadows raise their fists high.)

(HARRISON does the same, he holds the bloody handkerchief
in his fist.)

(Lights shift and swirl and turn dark, leaving a singular
spotlight resting on the swing set as it rocks back and forth.)

END OF PLAY

www.ingramcontent.com/pod-product-compliance
Lightning Source LLC
Chambersburg PA
CBHW052149090426
42741CB00010B/2201